Geography Activities

HOLT THE AMERICAN NATION IN THE MODERN ERA

HOLT, RINEHART AND WINSTON
A Harcourt Education Company
Austin • New York • Orlando • Atlanta • San Francisco • Boston • Dallas • Toronto • London

Cover: Christie's Images
Title Page: © CORBIS/Bill Ross

Printed in the United States of America

ISBN 0-03-065396-7

2 3 4 5 6 7 8 9 082 04 03 02

Geography Activities

Name ________________ Class ________ Date ________

CHAPTER 1

The New Nation

GEOGRAPHY ACTIVITY

BOSTON AT THE START OF THE REVOLUTION

The first battles of the Revolutionary War occurred in and around Boston, Massachusetts. Examine the map below, and answer the questions that follow.

The War Around Boston, 1773–1776

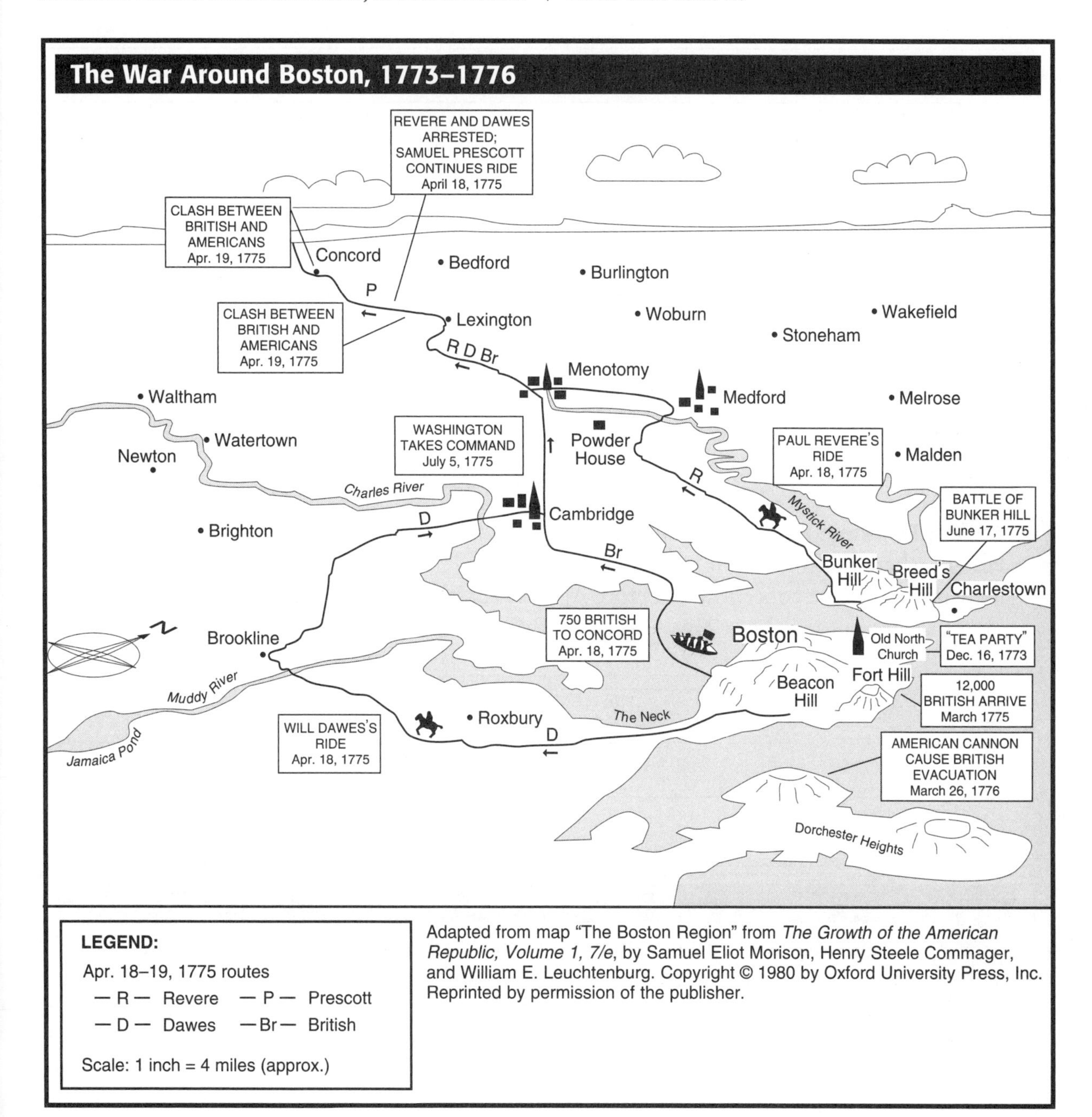

1. What is the first event shown on the map? What is the last event shown?

____

2. Approximately how far is Concord from the Old North Church?

____

3. What movements of April 18, 1775, are shown? What events took place on the day following these movements?

____

____

4. Describe the route the British traveled to get to Concord. Describe the route Paul Revere and William Dawes took.

____

____

____

5. Where is Bunker Hill located? Did the Battle of Bunker Hill take place before or after Washington took command?

____

6. **Critical Thinking: Places and Regions** Examine the map and locate the Powder House, where the colonial militia stored its gunpowder. Next, determine where British troops were concentrated before April 1775. Why might the militia have chosen to maintain the Powder House at this location?

____

____

____

ACTIVITY

Imagine that you are a newspaper reporter, and you are accompanying Paul Revere on his famous ride. In a short article for your paper, tell your readers what Revere did and why. You can use additional sources to provide details, such as the landscape, landmarks, and the weather. Share your article with the class.

Name ______________________ Class __________ Date __________

CHAPTER 2

The Expanding Nation

GEOGRAPHY ACTIVITY

The Louisiana Purchase

In 1803 representatives for President Thomas Jefferson attempted to purchase New Orleans and West Florida from the French for $10 million. Instead, the French government offered sole rights to the Mississippi River and the lands drained by its tributaries for $15 million. The U.S. envoys agreed, and in 1804 a mapping expedition was sent west under the leadership of William Clark and Meriwether Lewis. Examine the map of the Louisiana Purchase and the expedition, and answer the questions that follow.

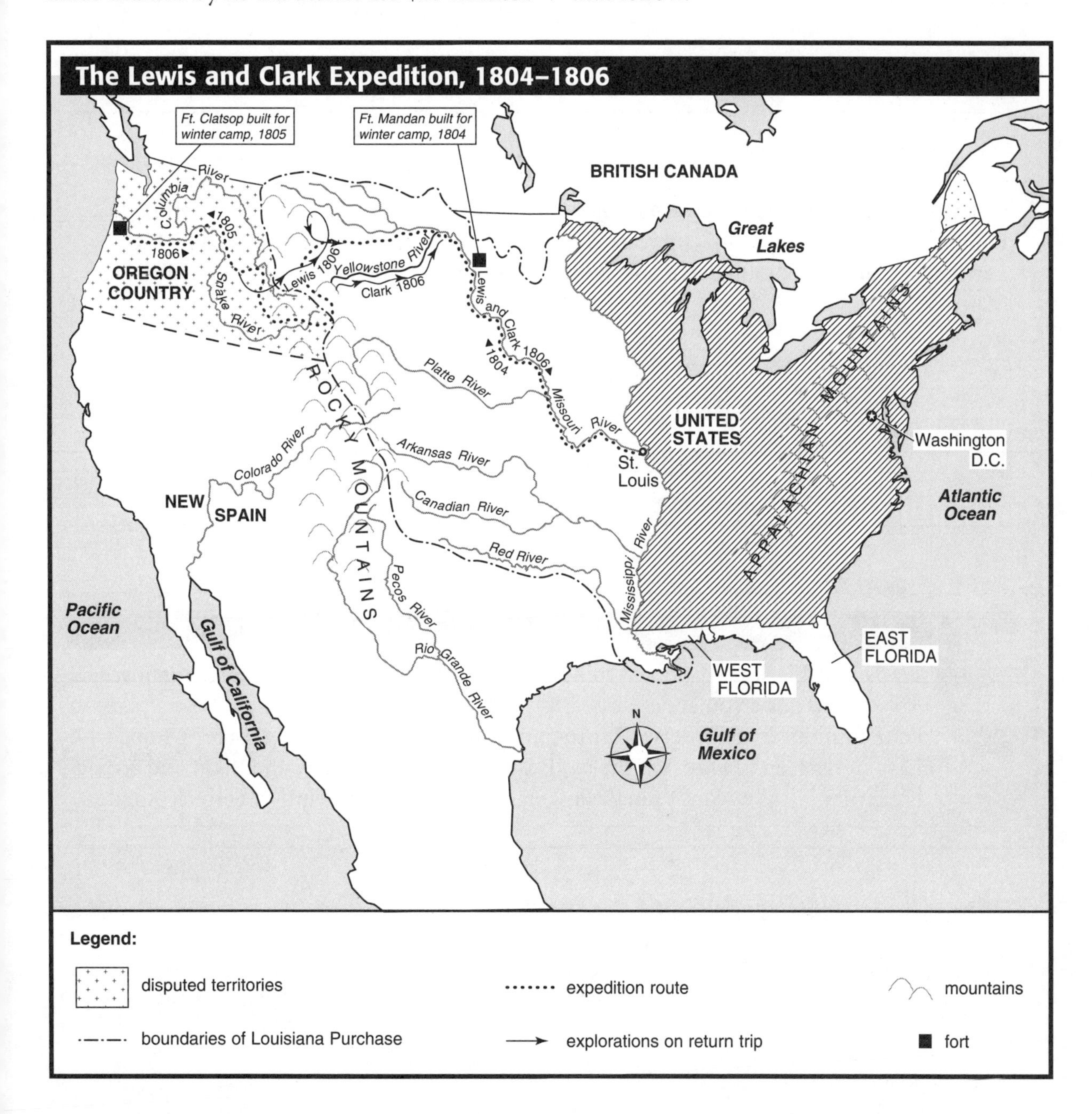

1. Where did Lewis and Clark begin their westward journey? Where did it end?

2. Where did they build their winter camp in 1804? What disputed territory did they travel through in 1805 and 1806?

3. Along what river did the expedition travel for most of the journey? What mountain range did it cross?

4. How did Clark's return route differ from the return route taken by Lewis?

5. **Critical Thinking: Human Systems** The Louisiana Purchase doubled the size of the United States. How might this increase in territory, and the knowledge gained by the Lewis and Clark expedition, have affected migration and settlement from the United States?

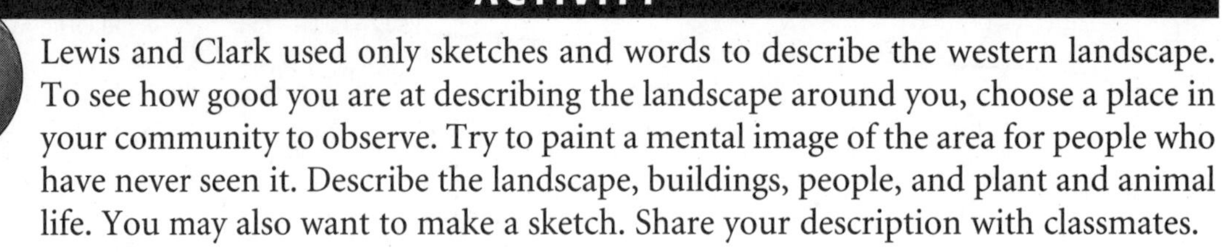

ACTIVITY

Lewis and Clark used only sketches and words to describe the western landscape. To see how good you are at describing the landscape around you, choose a place in your community to observe. Try to paint a mental image of the area for people who have never seen it. Describe the landscape, buildings, people, and plant and animal life. You may also want to make a sketch. Share your description with classmates.

Name ______________________ Class __________ Date __________

CHAPTER 3

The Civil War

GEOGRAPHY ACTIVITY

The Siege of Vicksburg

The fall of Vicksburg in July 1863 gave the Union effective control over the Mississippi River and brought an end to the Union campaign in the West. The map below shows the troop movements and battles that led up to the siege at Vicksburg, which began on May 17. Examine the map below, and answer the questions that follow.

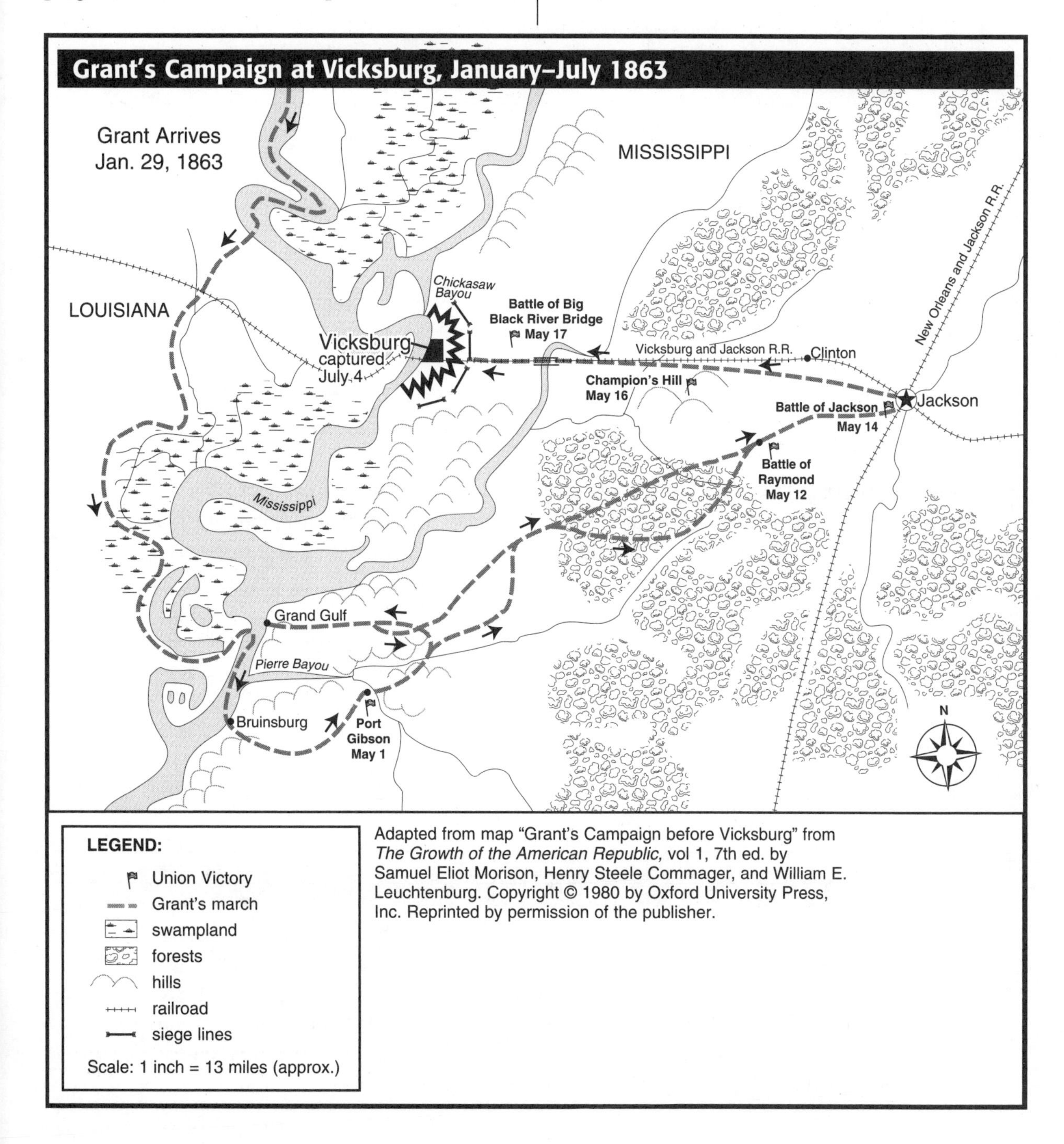

1. Describe Vicksburg's location and surrounding natural features.

2. In what state is Vicksburg located? What state is across the Mississippi River?

3. Describe Grant's approach to Vicksburg and the battles he fought during the campaign.

4. Why did Grant not attack Vicksburg from the north or from the west?

5. How long did Grant's campaign at Vicksburg last? Approximately how long was the actual siege?

6. **Critical Thinking: The Uses of Geography** Do you think the Union victory at Vicksburg was easy or difficult to achieve? Support your answer with evidence from the map, including geographic characteristics of the Vicksburg area and information on the battles. Do you think Grant chose his strategy wisely? Why or why not?

ACTIVITY

Controlling the Mississippi River was an important factor in winning the Union's western campaign. The Mississippi remains one of the United States's most important rivers—and one of its most spectacular. Make a one-page Fact List about the Mississippi River. Copy several photographs or illustrations to accompany the list. Working with class members, merge the Fact Lists and illustrations to create a comprehensive "Mighty Mississippi" bulletin board.

Name ________________ Class ________ Date ________

CHAPTER 4

Reconstruction and the New South

GEOGRAPHY ACTIVITY

Tenant Farming and Sharecropping

During Reconstruction, new patterns of farm labor developed in the South. Since slave labor was no longer available, many plantation owners chose to rent out parcels of land to tenant farmers, people who often were former slaves. Sharecropping—a variation on tenant farming in which farmers worked a parcel of land in exchange for a share of the crop, a cabin, seeds, tools, and a mule—also became widespread. The map below shows the extent of southern tenant farming in 1880. Examine the map, and answer the questions that follow.

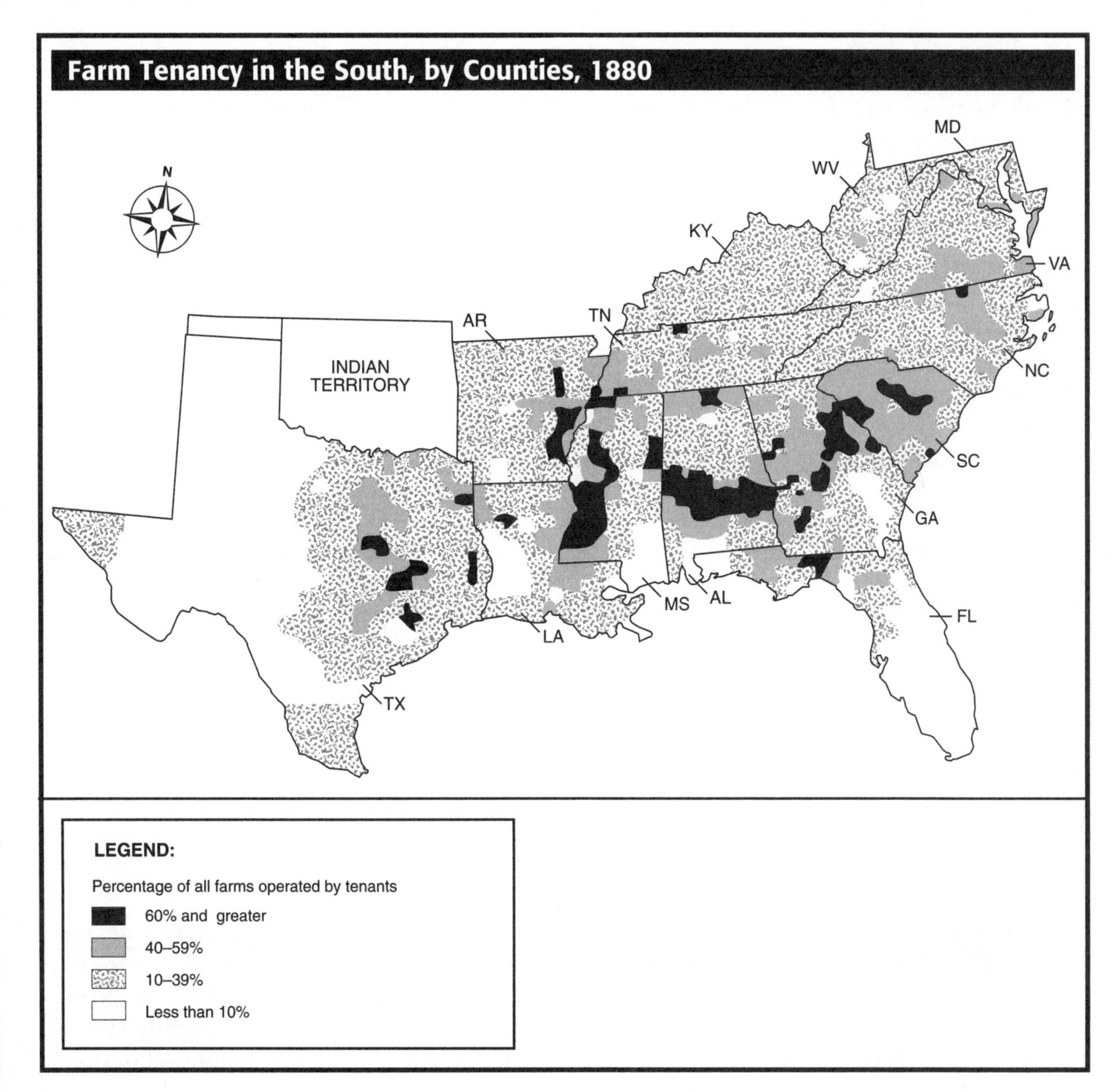

1. Name the state or territory in which tenants operated less than 10 percent of every county's farms in 1880.

2. What states had counties in which at least 60 percent of the farms were tenant operated?

3. Which two southern states appear to have had the highest percentage of tenant-operated farms? Which two states had large areas in which tenant farming was relatively uncommon?

4. Where was tenant farming less common: in the Deep South or in the western portion of the region? Based on your knowledge of the Cotton Kingdom, what might explain this trend?

5. **Critical Thinking: Places and Regions** By the outbreak of the Civil War, the center of the slave system had shifted from the Upper South to the cotton belt of the Deep South. How is this shift shown in this map, which illustrates farm tenancy patterns *after* the Civil War?

ACTIVITY

How much can a photograph tell you? Do library research to find a photograph or illustration of a sharecropper or tenant farmer during the late 1800s or early 1900s. Write an extended caption about the picture to tell the reader something about the work and lives of sharecroppers at that time.

Name ______________________ Class __________ Date __________

The Western Crossroads

GEOGRAPHY ACTIVITY

American Indian Lands in the West

During the last half of the 1800s, American Indians lost control over most of their western lands. The two maps below show changes in Indian-controlled territory. Examine the maps, and answer the questions that follow.

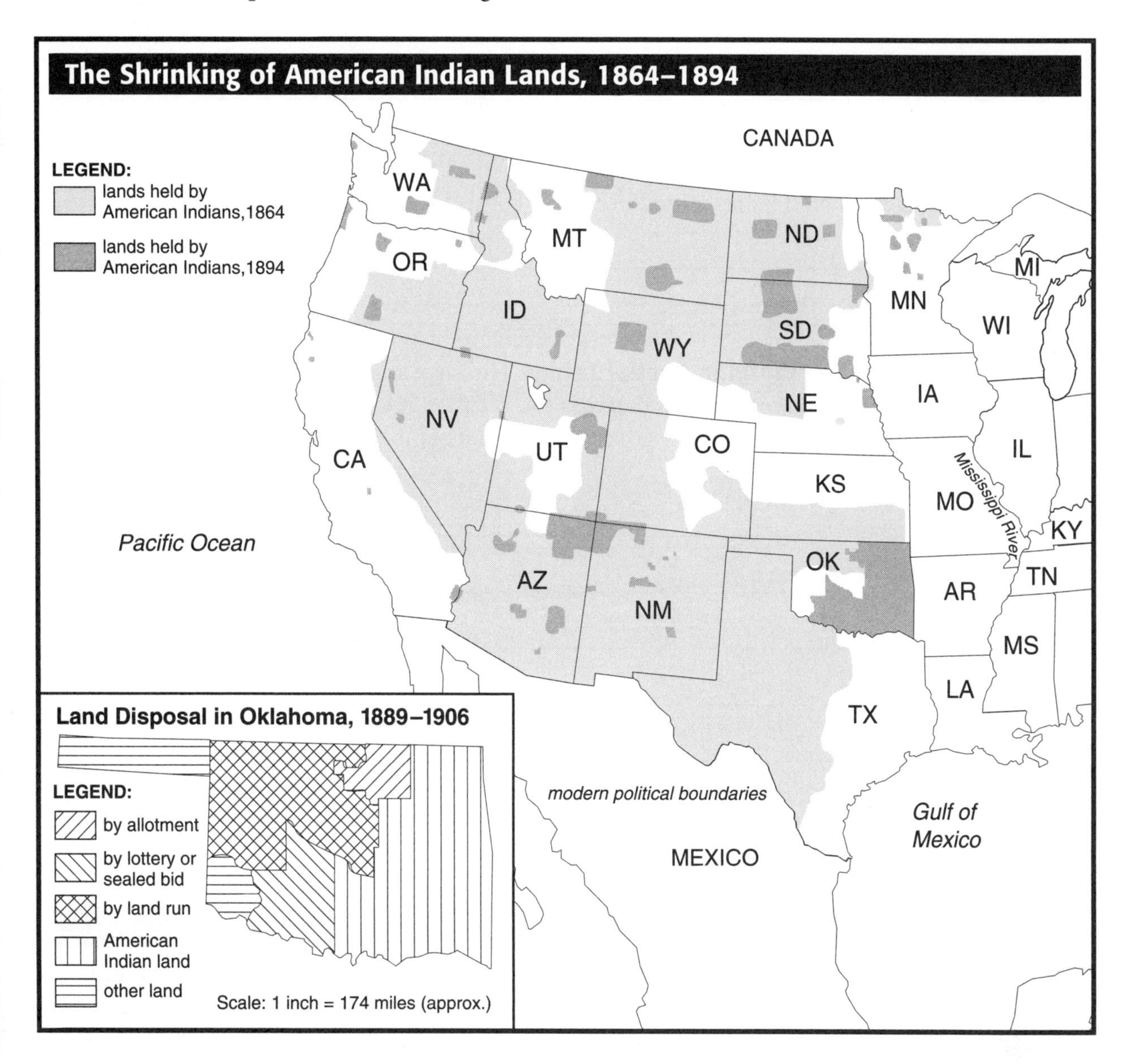

1. In which states west of the Mississippi River were no lands held by American Indians in 1864?

____

2. Which state was held entirely by American Indians in 1864? Which state had the most Indian-held lands in 1894?

____

3. Describe the changes in Indian land occupancy patterns between 1864 and 1894.

____

____

____

4. What portion of Oklahoma remained in Indian hands in 1906?

____

____

5. **Critical Thinking: The World in Spatial Terms** The large map indicates that in 1894 American Indians were scattered across the West on relatively small tracts of land. Why, in your opinion, did the government not assemble all American Indians in a single, large area?

____

____

____

____

____

____

ACTIVITY

Look for a map that shows the locations of American Indian reservations today. Draw the major ones on a map of your own. Compare your map with the 1884 map on this worksheet. Write a paragraph that explains the changes. Include a description of how American Indian land holdings in Oklahoma have changed.

Name ______________________ Class __________ Date __________

CHAPTER 6

The Second Industrial Revolution

GEOGRAPHY ACTIVITY

Pullman's Company Town

In 1880 George Pullman, the manufacturer of Pullman sleeping cars for railroads, built a company town near Chicago, Illinois. The town, which he named after himself, featured a factory and rail lines, as well as housing and other services for employees. In 1894 the town became the focus of one of the most bitter labor disputes in American history. Examine the maps and answer the questions that follow.

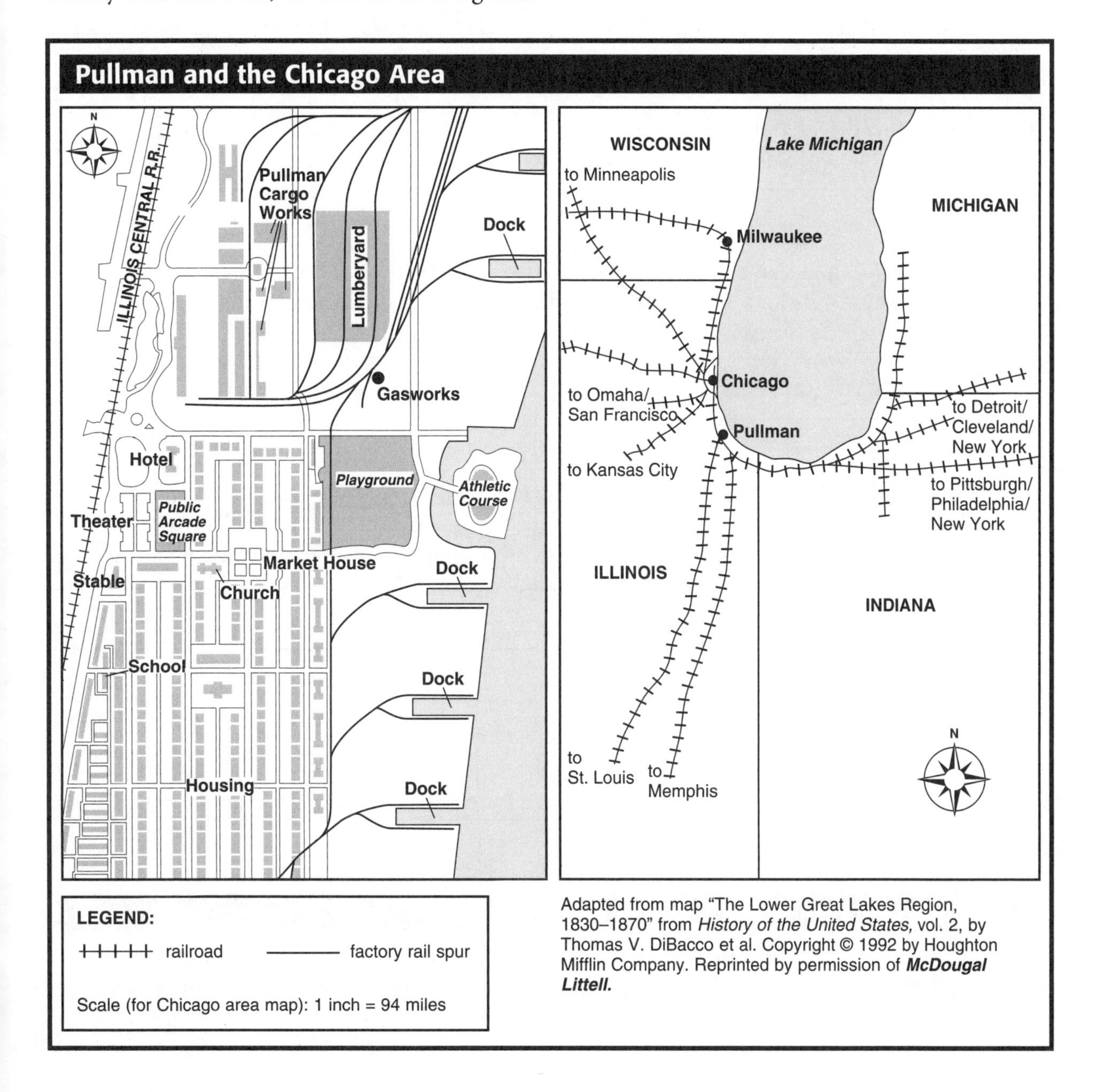

Adapted from map "The Lower Great Lakes Region, 1830–1870" from *History of the United States,* vol. 2, by Thomas V. DiBacco et al. Copyright © 1992 by Houghton Mifflin Company. Reprinted by permission of ***McDougal Littell.***

1. Where was the town of Pullman located?

2. On which side of town was the production area? Why might a railroad town have needed a lumberyard?

3. Where was the housing? What areas and buildings in the town were likely to be accessible to all of the residents and workers?

4. What rail line served Pullman? How else might supplies and finished products have been shipped in and out of town?

5. During the Pullman strike of 1894, sympathetic rail workers shut down many of the rail lines around Chicago. What effect does the map indicate this action might have had on the nation's transportation system?

6. **Critical Thinking: Human Systems** Initially, the town of Pullman was considered a model of enlightened management. Why might George Pullman have decided to build such a town? Examine the map for evidence of planned order and control and explain why workers might have found such an environment to be restrictive.

ACTIVITY

Research to learn more about the town of Pullman or about another company town from this era. Then draw four postcards that represent life in a company town.

Name ______________________ Class __________ Date __________

The Transformation of American Society

GEOGRAPHY ACTIVITY

Immigrant Groups in New York City

By 1900 some two million Russian, Irish, German, and Italian immigrants lived in New York City. These immigrants often clustered together by nationality, creating a patchwork quilt of ethnic neighborhoods across the city. The map below shows this pattern in the borough of Manhattan in 1910. Floor plans of a row of typical New York City tenement buildings are also shown. Examine the map and the diagram and answer the questions that follow.

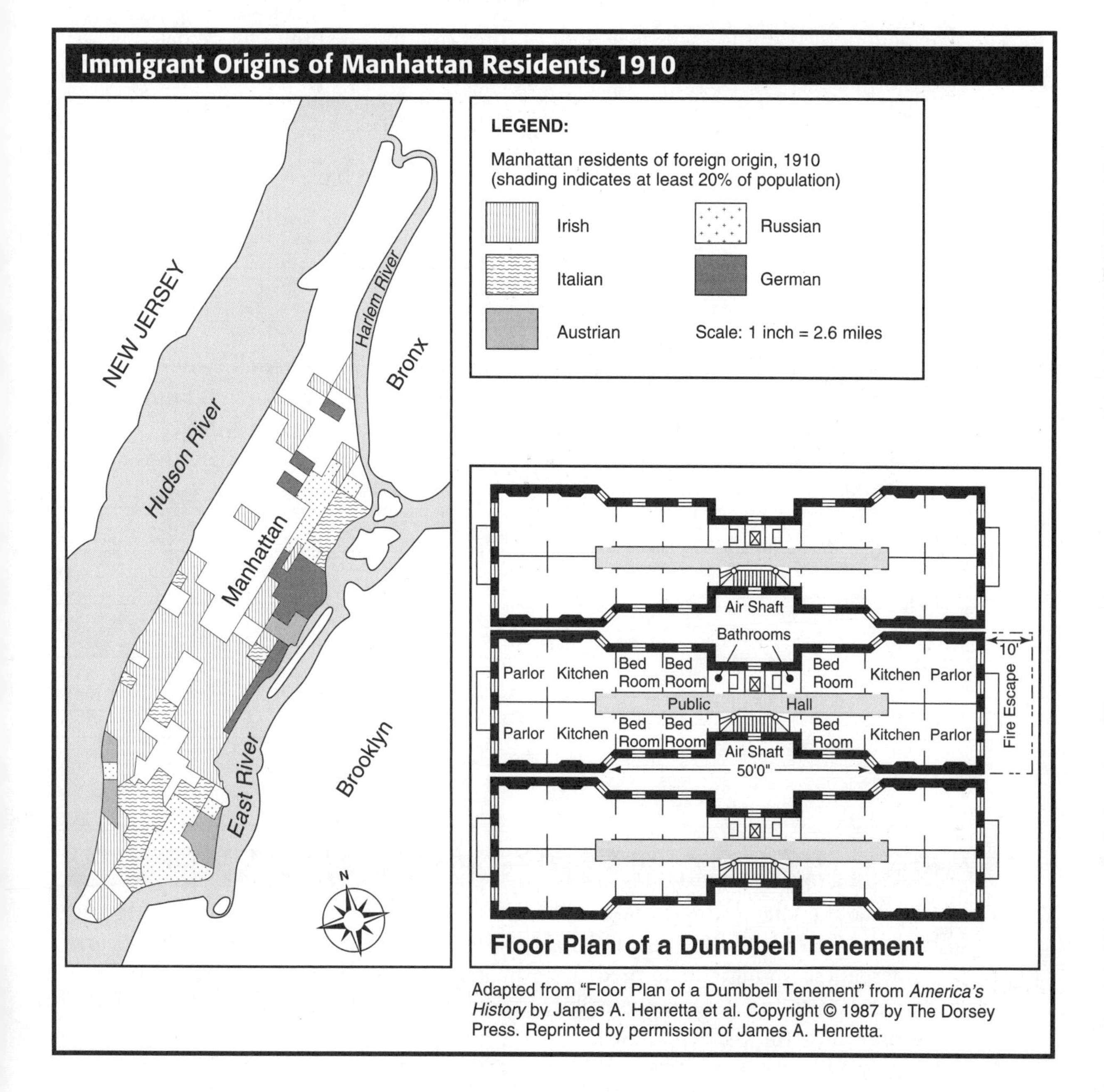

Adapted from "Floor Plan of a Dumbbell Tenement" from *America's History* by James A. Henretta et al. Copyright © 1987 by The Dorsey Press. Reprinted by permission of James A. Henretta.

1. What boroughs of New York City are labeled on the map? What state is labeled?

2. How long and wide is Manhattan? What national groups are shown there in 1910? What was the predominant immigrant group in Manhattan?

3. Where were Manhattan's nonimmigrant neighborhoods concentrated?

4. The tenement floor plan shows a single floor of three side-by-side buildings. What lay between each building? What emergency exits existed?

5. How many bathrooms were on each floor? Did each apartment have a bathroom? How can you determine the number of apartments?

6. **Critical Thinking: The World in Spatial Terms** Each floor of a "dumbbell" tenement, the kind shown in the diagram, was just 25 feet wide by 100 feet long. If four families lived on each floor, approximately how much space did each family have? What would be the drawbacks of living in such a place? What advantages might the community offer?

ACTIVITY

Review the chapter, and make a list of the immigrant groups that came to the United States between 1865 and 1910. Select one group, and do research to learn where these immigrants located. Then make a map of the United States with those areas shaded. In a paragraph, explore at least two reasons that may explain why the group chose this particular area.

Name ______________________ Class __________ Date __________

CHAPTER 8

Politics in the Gilded Age

GEOGRAPHY ACTIVITY

The Growth of Urban Areas

At the start of the 1800s, there were few large cities in the United States. But as industrialization and immigration increased during the latter part of the century, the urban population grew rapidly. The two maps below show how the level of urbanization in the United States changed between 1870 and 1920. Examine the two maps and answer the questions that follow.

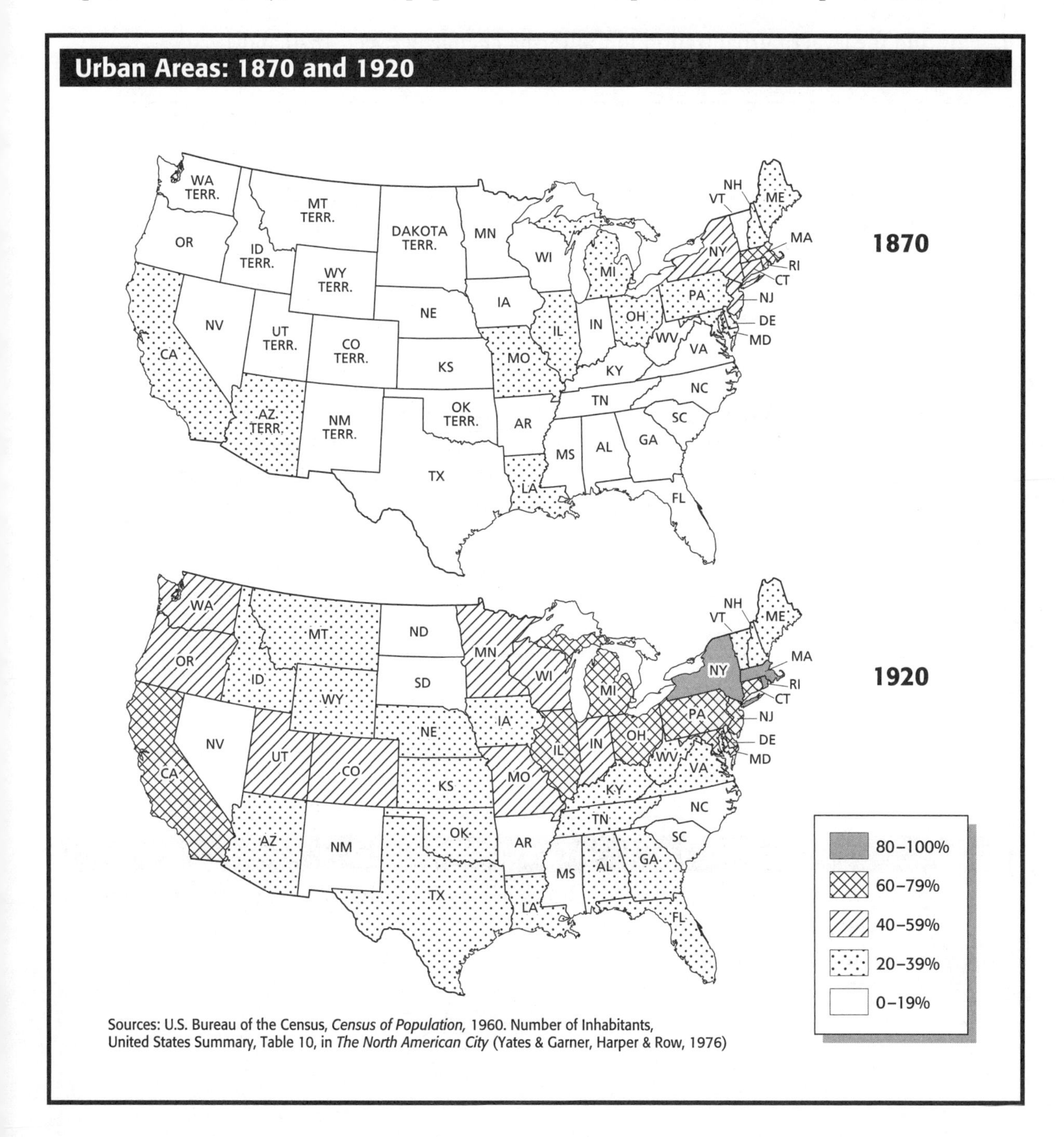

Sources: U.S. Bureau of the Census, *Census of Population,* 1960. Number of Inhabitants, United States Summary, Table 10, in *The North American City* (Yates & Garner, Harper & Row, 1976)

1. Which states had the highest level of urbanization in 1870?

2. Which states had the highest level of urbanization in 1920?

3. Which states remained the least urban in 1920? What was their level of urbanization?

4. How did the level of urbanization in California change between 1870 and 1920?

5. What can you conclude about the level of urbanization in the United States as a whole between 1870 and 1920? What forces might cause people to migrate westward over the years?

6. **Critical Thinking: Human Systems** According to the U.S. Census figures used for these maps, many states had a fairly high level of urbanization by 1920. Does this mean that there were large cities in all parts of these states? Think about the term, "level of urbanization," and explain how it is the best way to describe the change in population shown on these maps.

ACTIVITY

Do research to find a map that shows the level of urbanization of your state today. Investigate the forces that have caused some areas to grow and other areas to lose population. Write a paragraph about your findings.

Name ______________________________ Class __________ Date __________

The Age of Reform

GEOGRAPHY ACTIVITY

Limiting the Workday

During the early 1900s, progressive reformers and labor leaders supported legislation to limit the hours workers were required to spend on the job. The reformers hoped to reduce the average workday from 10 hours to 8 hours. The maps below show the progress made in the crusade for the eight-hour workday. Examine the maps, and answer the questions that follow.

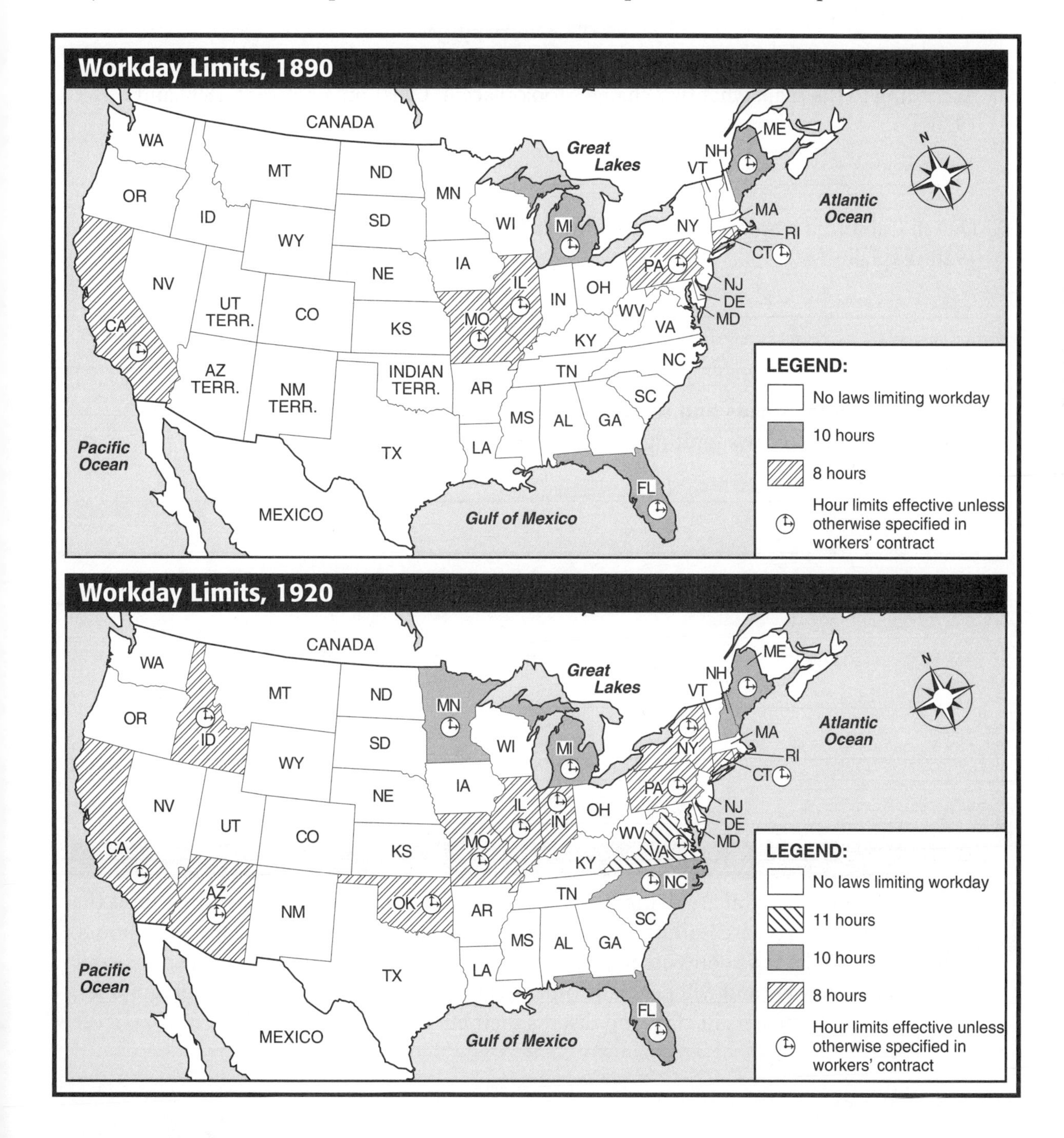

1. In 1890 how many states had laws limiting the workday? Which states were they?

____

____

2. Which states changed their workday laws between 1890 and 1920?

____

____

3. How did the workday laws change in Virginia between 1890 and 1920?

____

4. According to the map, what two changes took place in Oklahoma between 1890 and 1920?

____

5. Did all California employers have to limit their workday to eight hours in 1890? in 1920? Explain.

____

____

6. **Critical Thinking: Places and Regions** How might regional economies have influenced the passage of laws limiting the workday?

____

____

____

____

____

____

ACTIVITY

Imagine that you are living in 1920 in one of the states without laws that limit the workday. You are leading a movement to change the law to limit daily work hours. The public will soon vote to decide the issue. Create a poster that will express your point of view and will persuade others to vote as you would. Use text and graphics. Share the posters in class and discuss their effectiveness.

CHAPTER 10

Name ______________________ Class __________ Date __________

Progressive Politicians

GEOGRAPHY ACTIVITY

Theodore Roosevelt: A Biographical Map

Below is a list of events in the life of Theodore Roosevelt. Match the number of each event with the correct box on the map. Then answer the questions that follow.

List of Events

(1) — born in New York City, Oct. 27, 1858

(2) — graduates from Harvard University, Cambridge, 1880

(3) — serves in New York State Assembly, 1882–84

(4) — operates a ranch in North Dakota, 1884–86

(5) — returns to New York and serves as U.S. Civil Service Commissioner (1889–95) and president of New York City Board of Police Commissioners (1895–97)

(6) — appointed Assistant Secretary of the Navy (1897–98)

(7) — leads Rough Riders in Cuban Campaign during Spanish-American War, 1898

(8) — elected U.S. vice president, 1900; becomes president after assassination of McKinley in Sept. 1901; wins and serves full term as president, 1905–09

(9) — goes on expedition to Africa, returns with extensive selection of African wildlife, 1909–1910

(10) — splits with Republican Party in Chicago, June 1912; his supporters form Progressive Party

(11) — survives assassination attempt in Milwaukee, Oct. 1912

(12) — explores Brazilian Amazon, 1913–14

(13) — dies at Oyster Bay, New York (Long Island), June 6, 1919

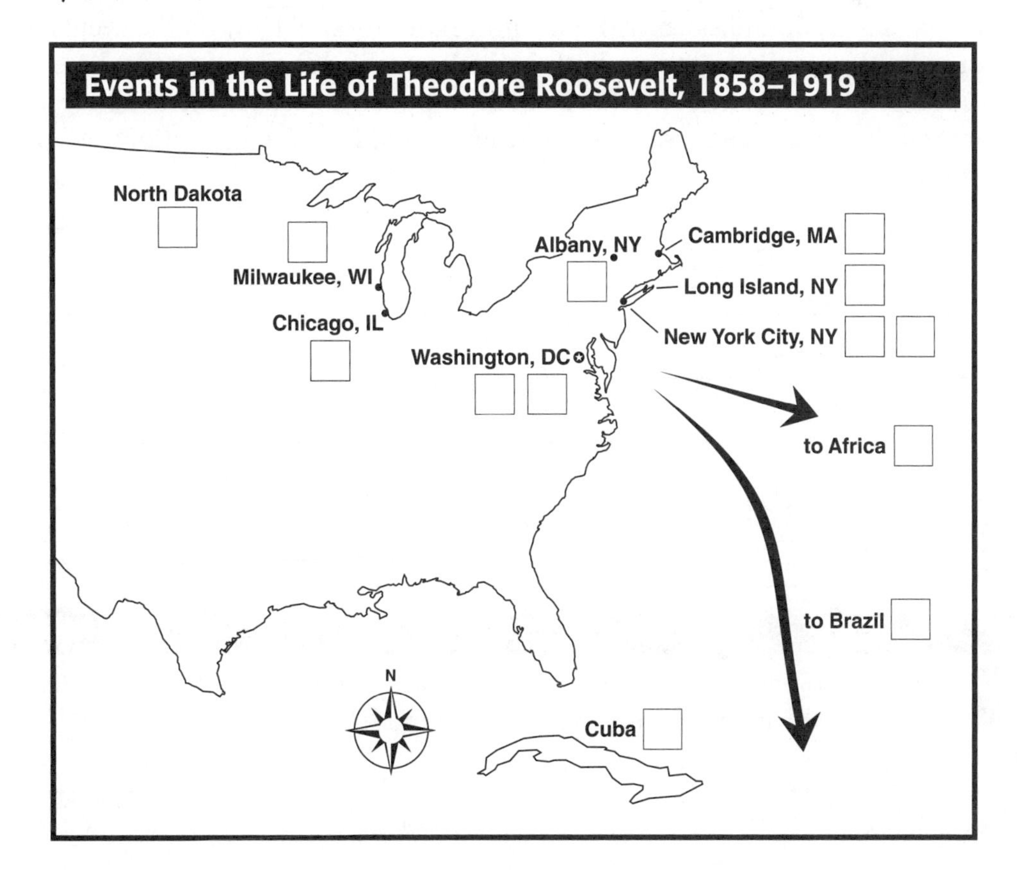

1. When was Roosevelt born? How old was he when he died?

2. Where did Roosevelt go to college? What was the first elected position he held?

3. Why did he leave the country in 1898? What other two foreign trips are noted on the map?

4. When was Roosevelt a rancher? Where was his ranch?

5. How long did he serve as president?

6. When did Roosevelt and his supporters form the Progressive Party? What danger did Roosevelt face several months later?

7. **Critical Thinking: Environment and Society** Historians have noted that Theodore Roosevelt possessed boundless energy and enthusiasm for life. How do the events on the map reflect Roosevelt's interests, both in intellectual fields and in physical arenas? Do you think the country benefits from having such an active, energetic president, or is a calm, reflective personality more appropriate to lead the nation? Support your answer.

ACTIVITY

Create a biographical map of a famous historical figure of the late 1800s or early 1900s. Use the map on this worksheet as a model.

Name ______________________ Class __________ Date __________

America and the World

GEOGRAPHY ACTIVITY

Foreign Powers in China, 1911

The growing influence of foreign powers over China prompted the United States to issue the Open Door policy in 1899 in an effort to ensure continued American access to Chinese trade. The following year the Boxer Rebellion revealed the depth of Chinese anger at all foreign presence in China. In 1911, however, large areas of China remained under the influence or direct control of imperialist powers. Examine the map and answer the questions that follow.

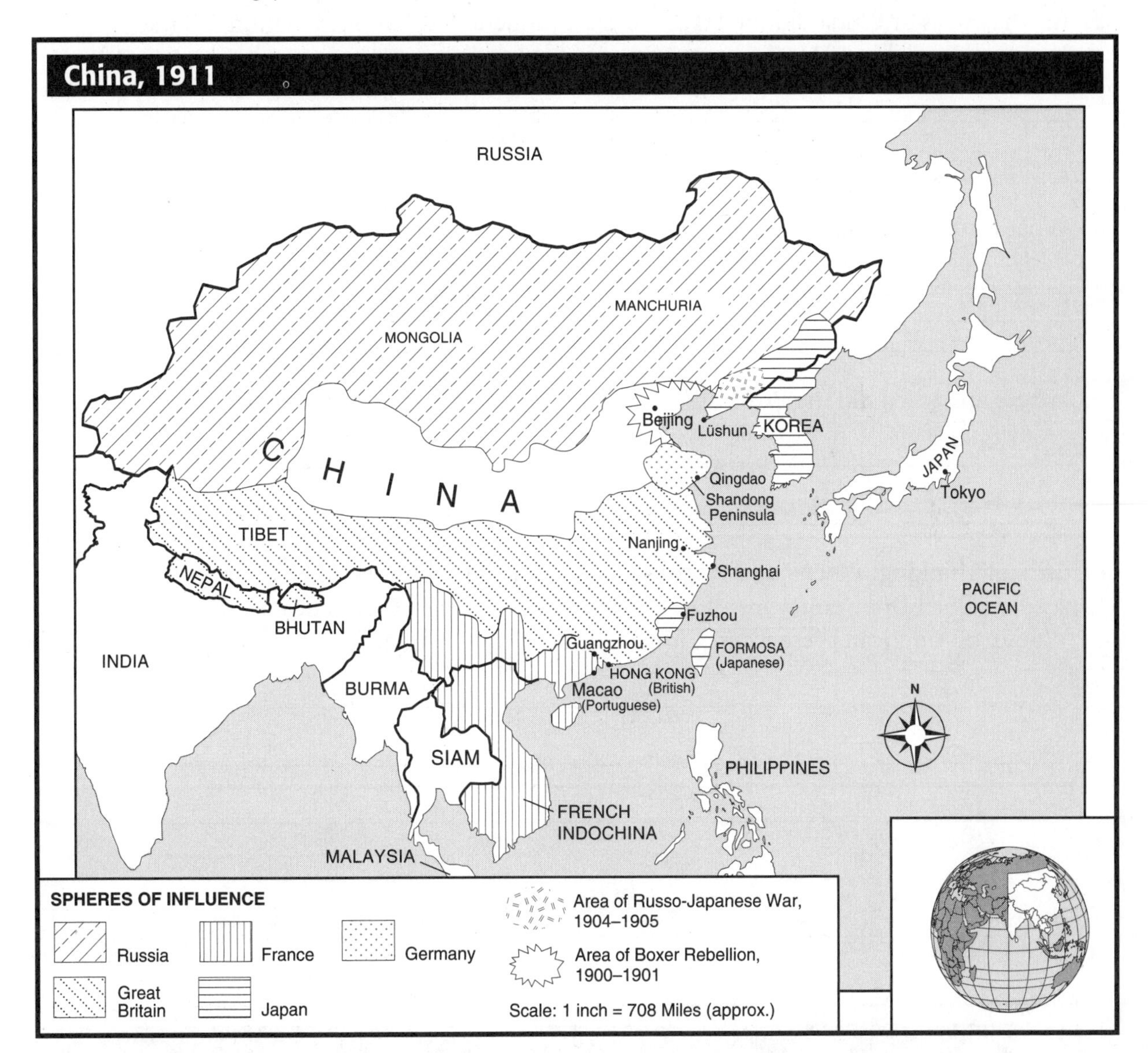

1. What foreign powers had spheres of influence in China in 1911? Which sphere of influence was the largest? Which was the smallest?

2. What geographic feature was in the German sphere of influence? What port did the Germans control?

3. In what areas of China did the Japanese exert influence? What other nation did the Japanese control in 1911?

4. What three major ports were clustered in southeast China? Who controlled them?

5. Where and when did the Boxer Rebellion and Russo-Japanese War take place?

6. **Critical Thinking: Places and Regions** Why do you think the United States pursued an Open Door policy instead of establishing a sphere of influence in China? Would an American presence in China have been in U.S. interests? Why or why not?

ACTIVITY

Consult a current map to see how the boundaries in this area of Asia have changed. Draw a map that compares the 1911 boundaries with those of today.

Name ______________________ Class __________ Date __________

World War I

GEOGRAPHY ACTIVITY

World War I

The countries that took part in World War I committed millions of troops to the fighting and suffered heavy casualties. The map below provides information on the numbers of troops contributed by the various nations fighting on both sides of the war. Examine the map and answer the questions that follow.

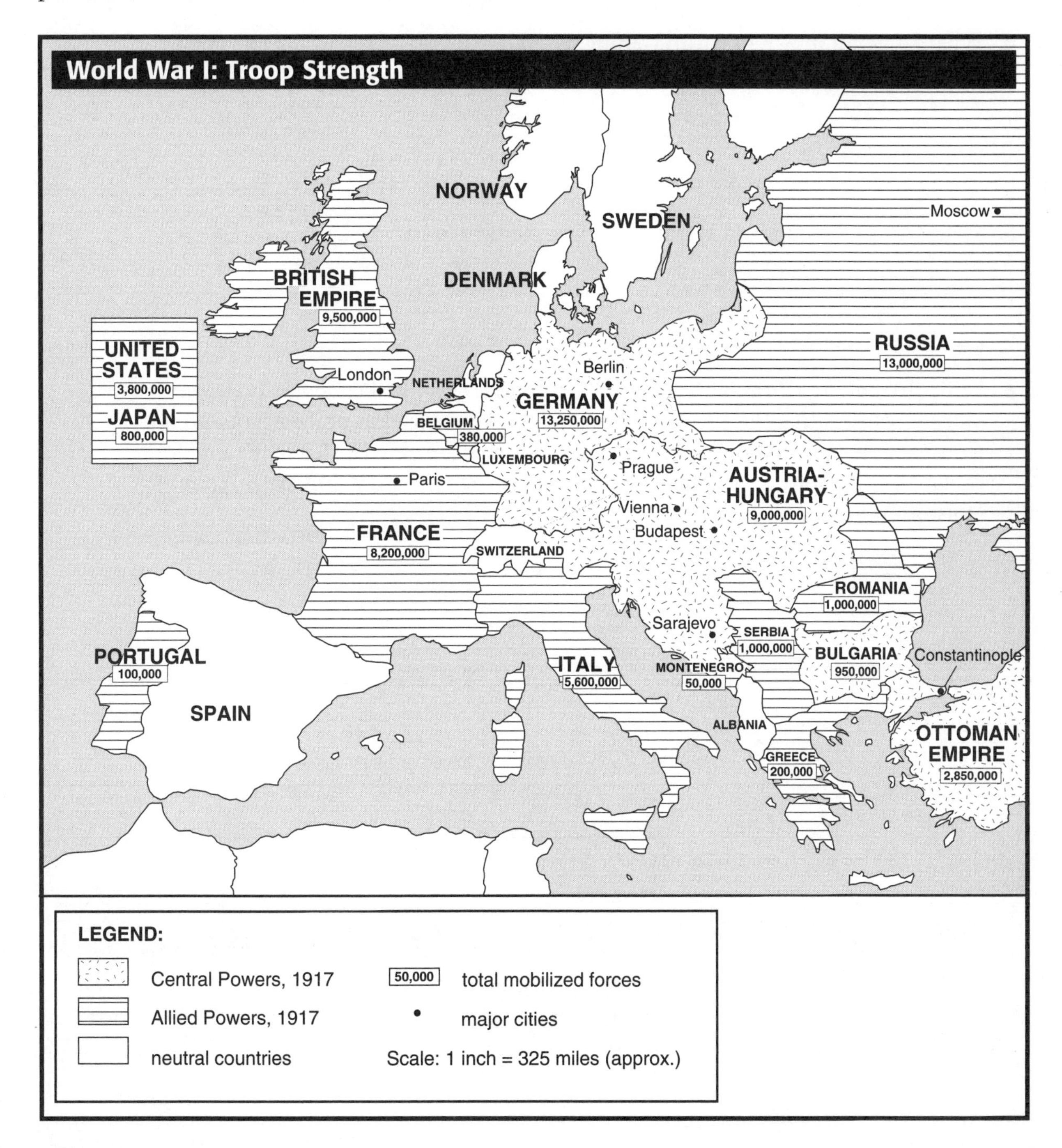

1. Which countries belonged to the Allied Powers?

2. Which countries belonged to the Central Powers?

3. Which European countries remained neutral in the war?

4. What cities are shown in Austria-Hungary? What city is shown in the Ottoman Empire?

5. Which countries supplied at least 1 million soldiers to the war?

6. Critical Thinking: Human Systems After World War I had ended, Woodrow Wilson believed that the United States should take the lead in peace negotiations. Compare the information about troop commitment for the United States and for other Allied nations. What factors caused Europeans to be unenthusiastic about Wilson's peace plan?

ACTIVITY

Several countries remained neutral during World War I. Choose one from the map. Do research to find out why that country refused to choose sides. Write two or three paragraphs on what you find.

Name ______________________ Class __________ Date __________

A Turbulent Decade

GEOGRAPHY ACTIVITY

The Republican Decade

Republican presidential candidates emerged victorious throughout the 1920s. The maps below show the results of the presidential elections during that decade. Examine the maps and answer the questions that follow.

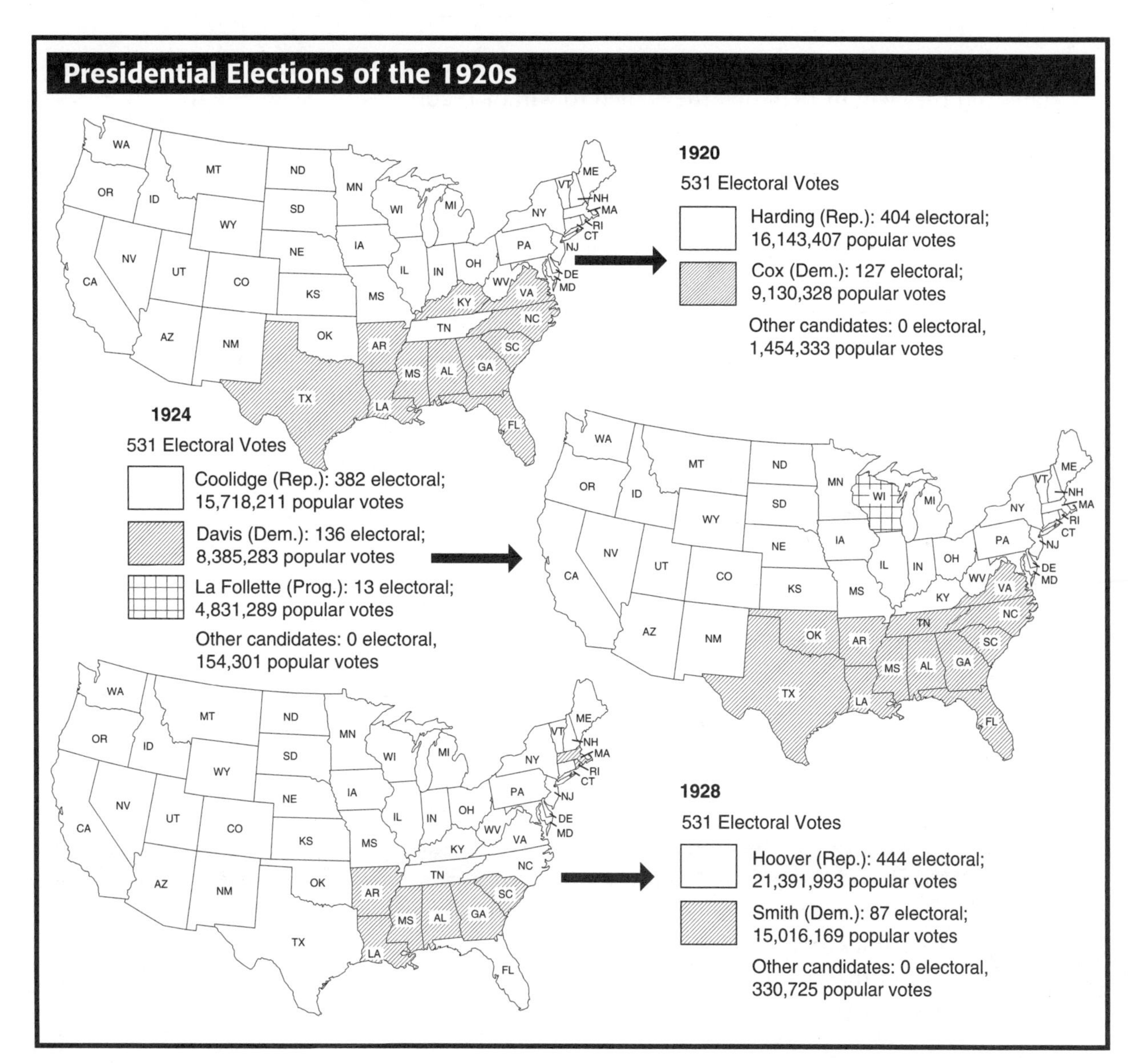

1. Who won the elections of 1920, 1924, and 1928? Which of these candidates enjoyed the widest margin of victory in electoral votes? Whose margin of victory was greatest in popular votes?

____

____

2. In general, which parts of the country voted for Republican presidential candidates during the 1920s? Where did the Democrats generally fare best?

____

3. Which state did the Democrats win in 1920 that they did not win in 1924? Which states did they win in 1924 that they failed to win in 1920?

____

4. Who was the third candidate in 1924? What state did he win and how many votes—both electoral and popular—did he receive?

____

5. **Critical Thinking: The Uses of Geography** Compare the popular vote counts for the Democratic Party in each of the three elections. Then compare the electoral vote counts for the Democratic Party in each election. What conclusion can you draw about the relationship between electoral votes and popular votes?

____

____

____

____

____

ACTIVITY

Draw a map of the United States, including the state boundaries. Indicate with colors whether each state's electoral votes went to the Democratic Party or Republican Party in the last presidential election. Write a paragraph that explains where the votes of each party were concentrated, and contrast this with "The Republican Decade."

Name ______________________ Class ____________ Date ____________

The Jazz Age

GEOGRAPHY ACTIVITY

The Prohibition Era

During the 1920s, the era of prohibition, thousands of Americans were arrested for the possession or sale of alcohol. By 1929 the illegal trade in alcohol showed no signs of slowing down. The maps below show alcohol-related arrests and seizures of distilling equipment in 1929. Examine the maps and answer the questions that follow.

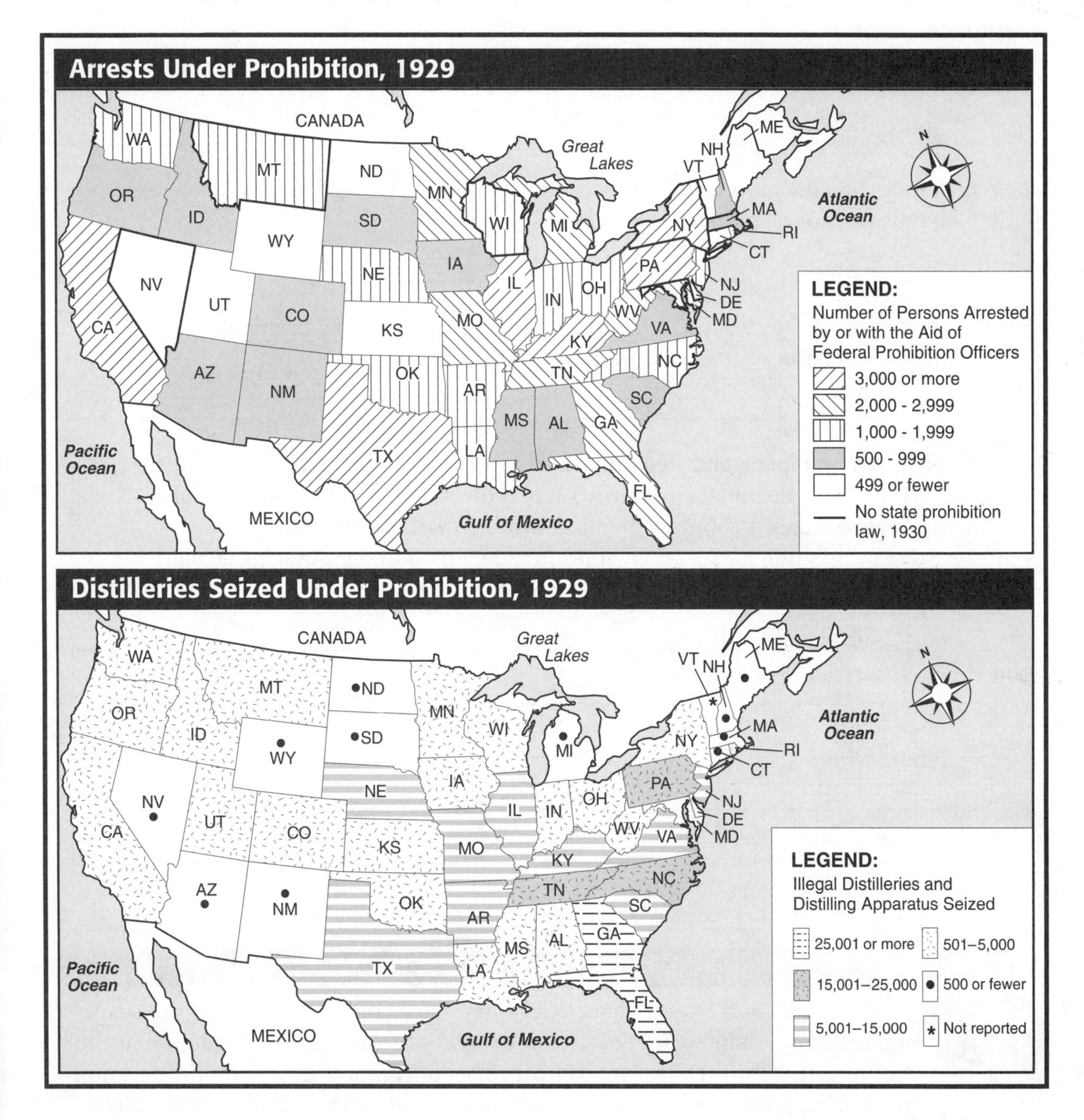

1. Which states had 3,000 or more alcohol-related arrests in 1929? Which of those states had more than 5,000 seizures of illegal distilleries or distilling equipment?

____

2. In 1929, which states had fewer than 500 alcohol-related arrests? Which of those states had 500 or fewer distilleries seized?

____

____

3. Where were there no state prohibition laws in 1930? Which of those states had 2,000 or more arrests in 1929?

____

____

4. Which states had the most distilleries seized? Approximately how many were seized? Which state did not report such information?

____

5. Were more people arrested in the East or in the West for breaking prohibition laws? Were more distilleries seized in the East or in the West?

____

6. **Critical Thinking: Places and Regions** Assess the information conveyed in these two maps. What do the number of arrests across the nation and the influence of gangs in Chicago suggest about the public attitude toward prohibition? Do you believe that prohibition laws were an appropriate method of discouraging alcohol consumption?

____

____

____

____

____

ACTIVITY

Local libraries and historical societies often have collections of local newspapers published over many years. Search these sources to learn about prohibition in your state or community. Draw a map of your state or community pinpointing locations mentioned in the article. Label the locations with the events that occurred there.

Name ______________________ Class __________ Date __________

The Great Depression

GEOGRAPHY ACTIVITY

Public Unrest During the Depression

During the 1930s, labor organization and unrest increased in response to the harsh conditions of the Great Depression. The map below indicates major strikes and union membership by state. Examine the map and answer the questions that follow.

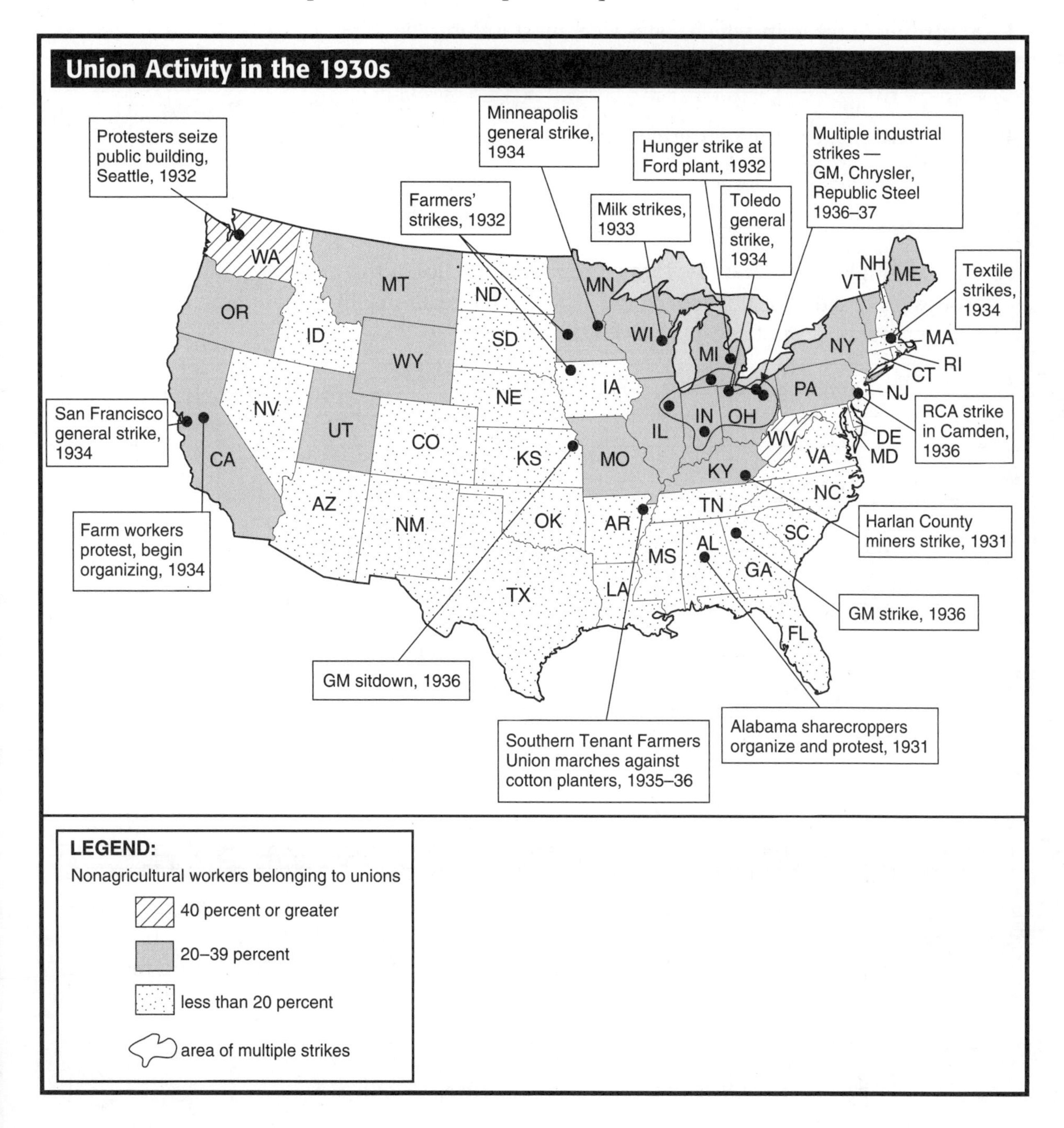

1. What major strike took place in Kentucky? What farm strikes or protests does the map show?

____

____

2. Where did the RCA strike take place? What major strikes occurred in Kansas and Georgia?

____

3. According to the map, which states were most unionized?

____

4. What percentage of the nonagricultural workforce was unionized in Missouri, Montana, and Tennessee?

____

5. **Critical Thinking: Human Systems** From the evidence in the map, what different groups protested or struck during the 1930s? What relationship do you think existed between public protest and the Great Depression?

____

____

____

____

____

____

____

____

ACTIVITY

Search newspapers and magazines to find a protest or strike that occurred in your state during the past 10 years. Draw its location on a map of your state. In a paragraph or two, explain the disagreement and express your point of view on the issue.

Name ______________________ Class __________ Date __________

CHAPTER 16

The New Deal

GEOGRAPHY ACTIVITY

The Public Works Administration

The Public Works Administration (PWA) was a New Deal agency created in 1933 to help fund major construction projects. Its goal, in part, was to reduce unemployment and promote economic recovery. The PWA provided federal funds (often matched by state and local contributions) for public works such as dams, schools, bridges, and water treatment plants. The map below shows the number and variety of PWA projects underway in 1938. Examine the map, and answer the questions that follow.

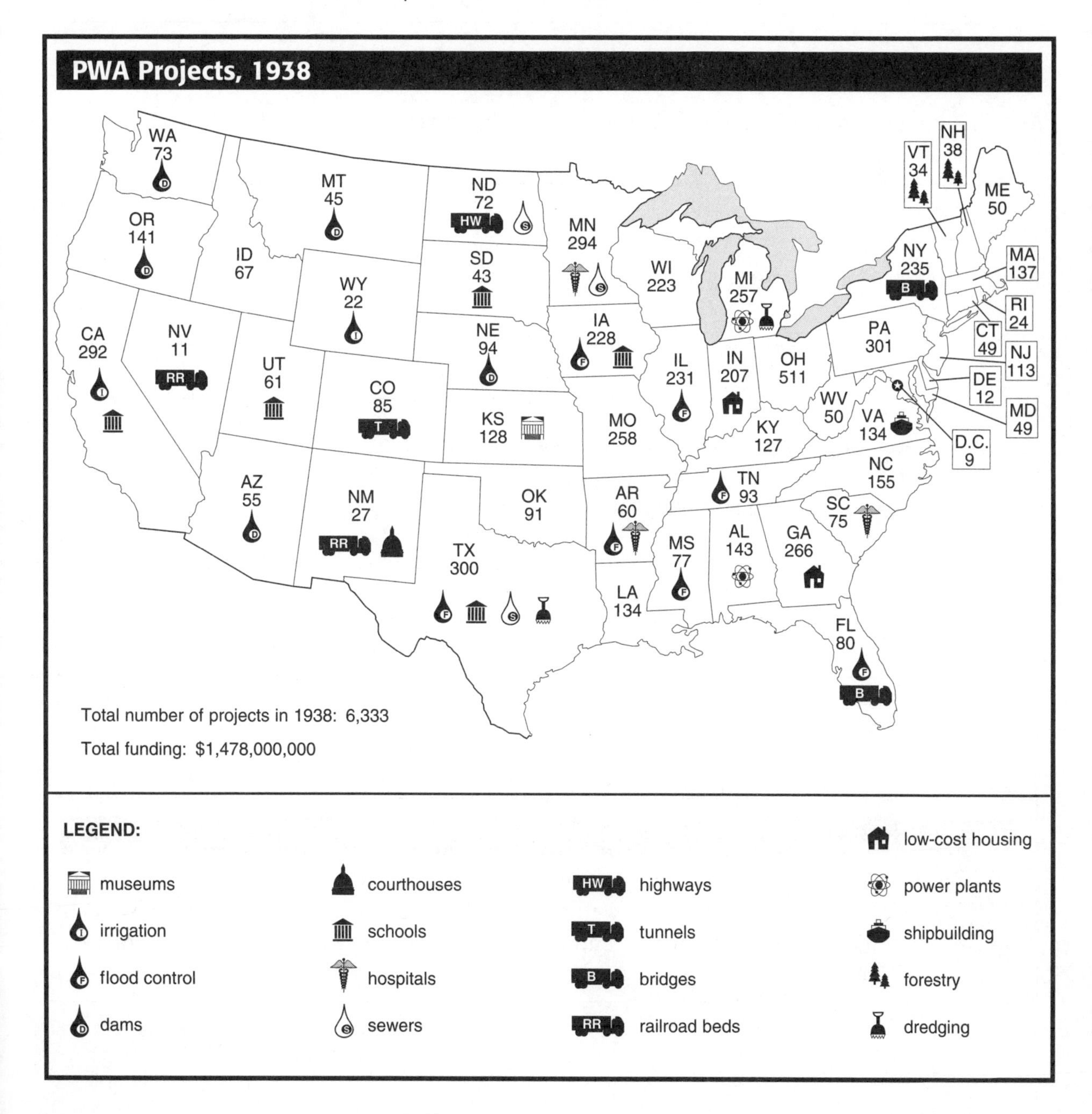

1. How many PWA projects were underway nationwide in 1938?

____

2. How many projects were underway in the District of Columbia in 1938?

____

3. Which state had the most projects underway in 1938? Which state had the fewest?

____

4. How did California compare with New York in number of projects? What kind of projects were undertaken in California?

____

____

5. What kind of projects are noted for Georgia and Indiana?

____

____

6. In what states did the PWA help build schools?

____

____

7. **Critical Thinking: Environment and Society** Look at the kinds of PWA projects listed on the map. How might these projects have affected people directly? How might these projects have stimulated a local economy?

____

____

____

____

ACTIVITY

If the PWA existed today, what useful jobs could it do in your state or community? Describe a project that a modern PWA might undertake. Explain why such a project should be chosen, and explain the good it would do in your state or community.

Name ______________________ Class __________ Date __________

CHAPTER 17

The Road to War

GEOGRAPHY ACTIVITY

The Good Neighbor Policy

During the 1930s the United States adopted the Good Neighbor Policy in an effort to promote cooperative, friendly relations with Latin America. Nevertheless, the United States continued to exert a controlling influence over the region. The map below shows key developments in U.S. relations with Central America and the Caribbean during the 1930s. Examine the map, and answer the questions that follow.

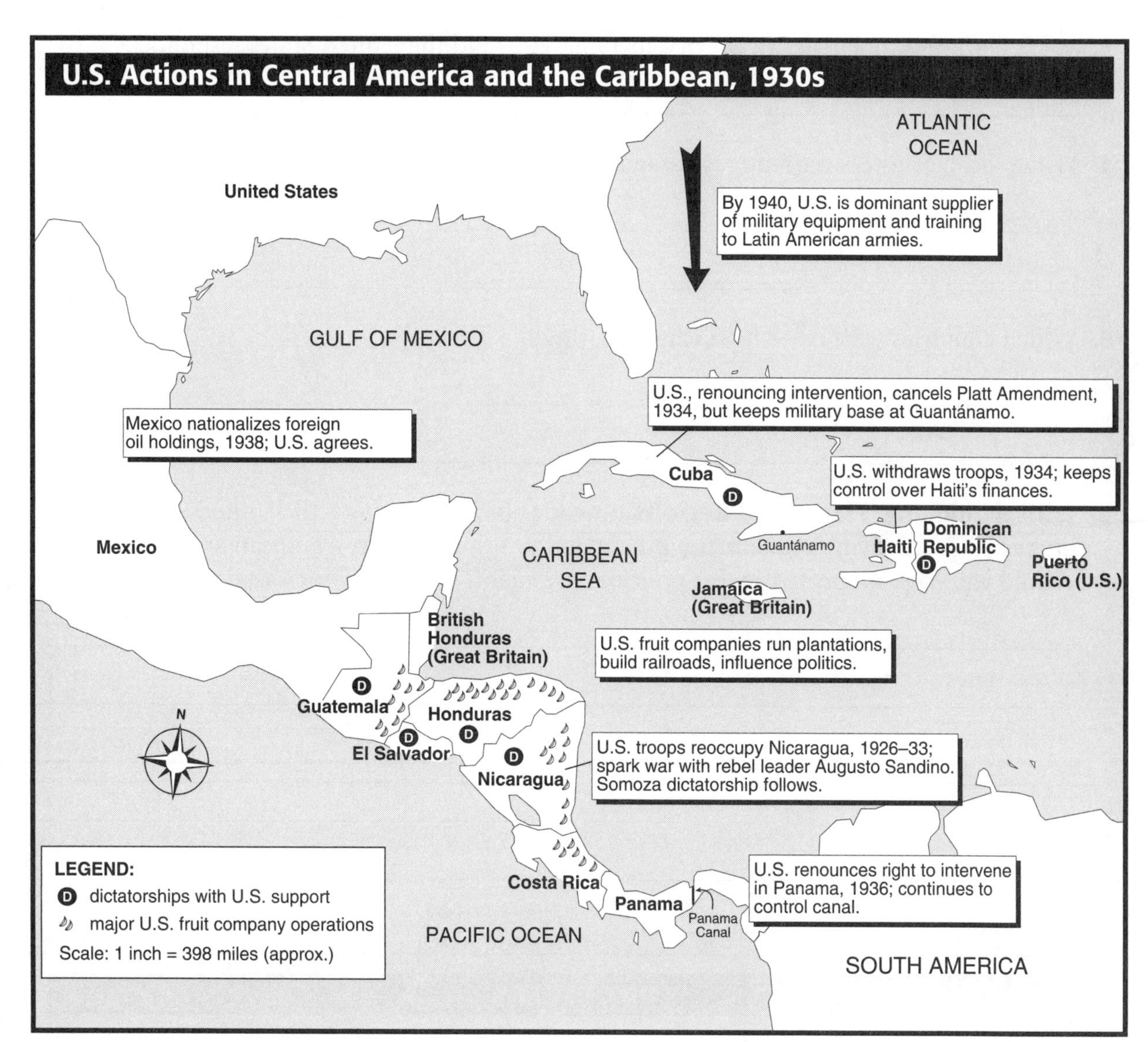

1. List the Central American and Caribbean countries shown on the map.

____

____

2. What gestures did the United States make toward Cuba and Panama during this period? How were those actions similar?

____

____

____

3. What key event took place in Mexico in 1938? How did the United States respond?

____

4. When did U.S. forces reoccupy Nicaragua? What happened as a result?

____

____

5. Which countries were ruled by dictators during this period?

____

____

6. Critical Thinking: Places and Regions In your opinion, why was the United States interested in supplying military equipment and training to Latin American armies? Would you have supported such a policy as president?

____

____

____

____

____

ACTIVITY

American influence in Latin America continues today. Choose one of the Latin American countries on the map, then find a photograph or illustration that shows American influence on its popular culture. Write an extended caption that explains how the photograph or illustration shows American cultural influence.

Name ______________________ Class __________ Date __________

CHAPTER 18

Americans in World War II

GEOGRAPHY ACTIVITY

Hitler's War Machine

Germany's early success in World War II brought most of Europe under Axis control. In addition to the Axis nations and their satellites (puppet governments), most of Europe was ruled directly by Germany or occupied by German forces in control of local governments. Only a small portion of Europe and North Africa was controlled by the Allies. The map below shows Axis and Allied occupation in 1942. Examine the map, and answer the questions that follow.

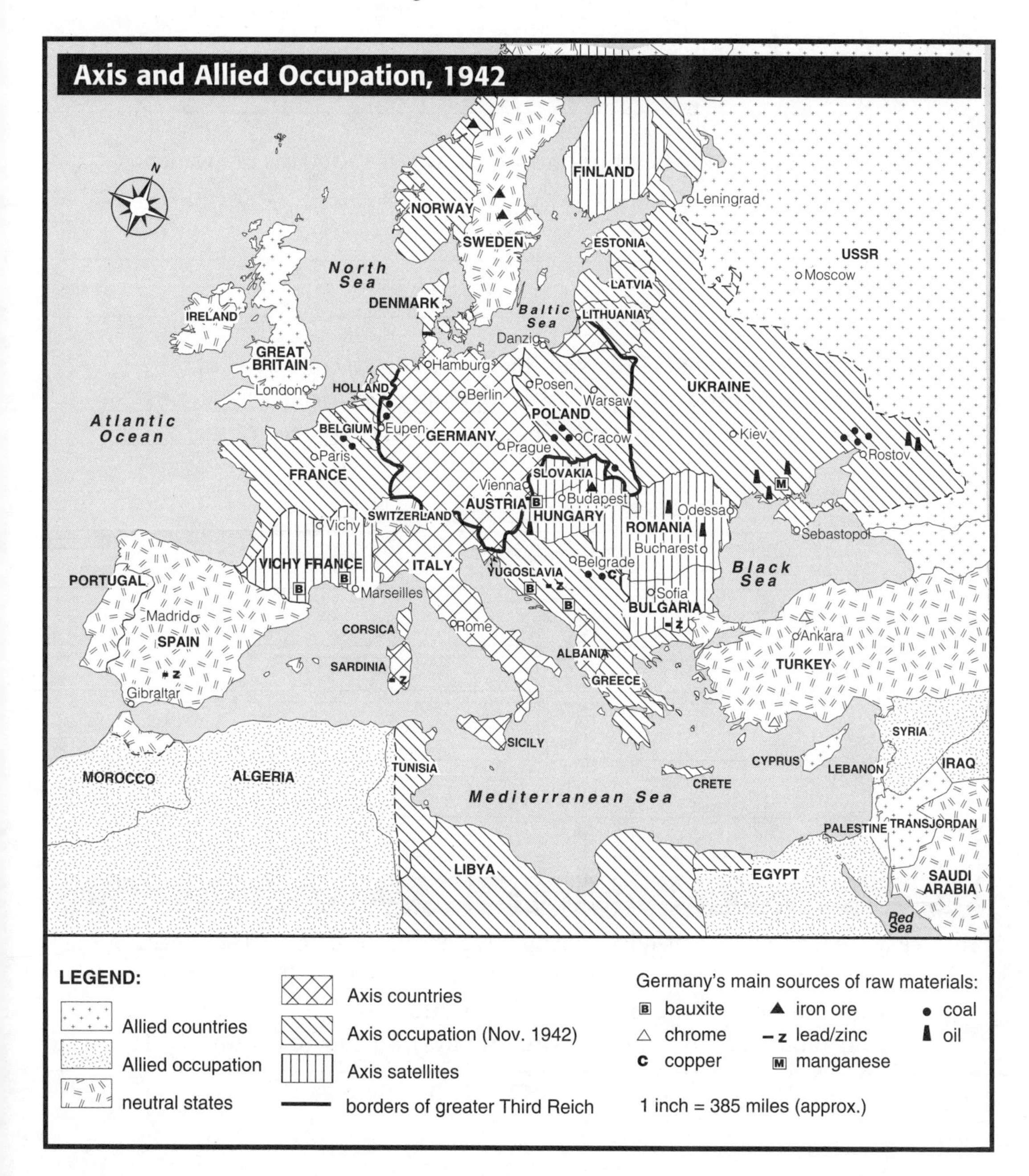

1. What Allied nations or Allied-occupied lands are shown on this map?

____

____

2. Which countries were Axis satellites? What raw materials did they provide to Germany?

____

____

3. What mineral did the Germans obtain from Poland? From what area were the Germans able to get manganese?

____

____

4. What neutral country existed in the heart of Europe? How was the status of Sweden different from that of Norway?

____

____

5. **Critical Thinking: Human Systems** Hitler's ultimate goal was to control all of Europe. How does the map illustrate his efforts? Is it possible for a leader to successfully impose his or her own rule over an unwilling population composed of many diverse peoples?

____

____

____

____

____

____

ACTIVITY

Interview someone who was alive during 1942 about his or her experiences in the military or on the home front during World War II. As a result of Germany's early successes in Europe, did the person fear that Hitler would succeed? Record the interview on audiotape (no more than 10 minutes), and share it with the class.

Name ______________ Class ________ Date ________

CHAPTER 19

The Cold War

GEOGRAPHY ACTIVITY

Postwar Tensions in the Eastern Mediterranean

One of the crisis areas in the postwar world was the eastern Mediterranean. In 1947 the threat of Soviet expansion in this region caused President Truman to issue the Truman Doctrine, pledging support for efforts to resist the spread of communism. The map below shows the region and notes several points of conflict. Examine the map, and answer the questions that follow.

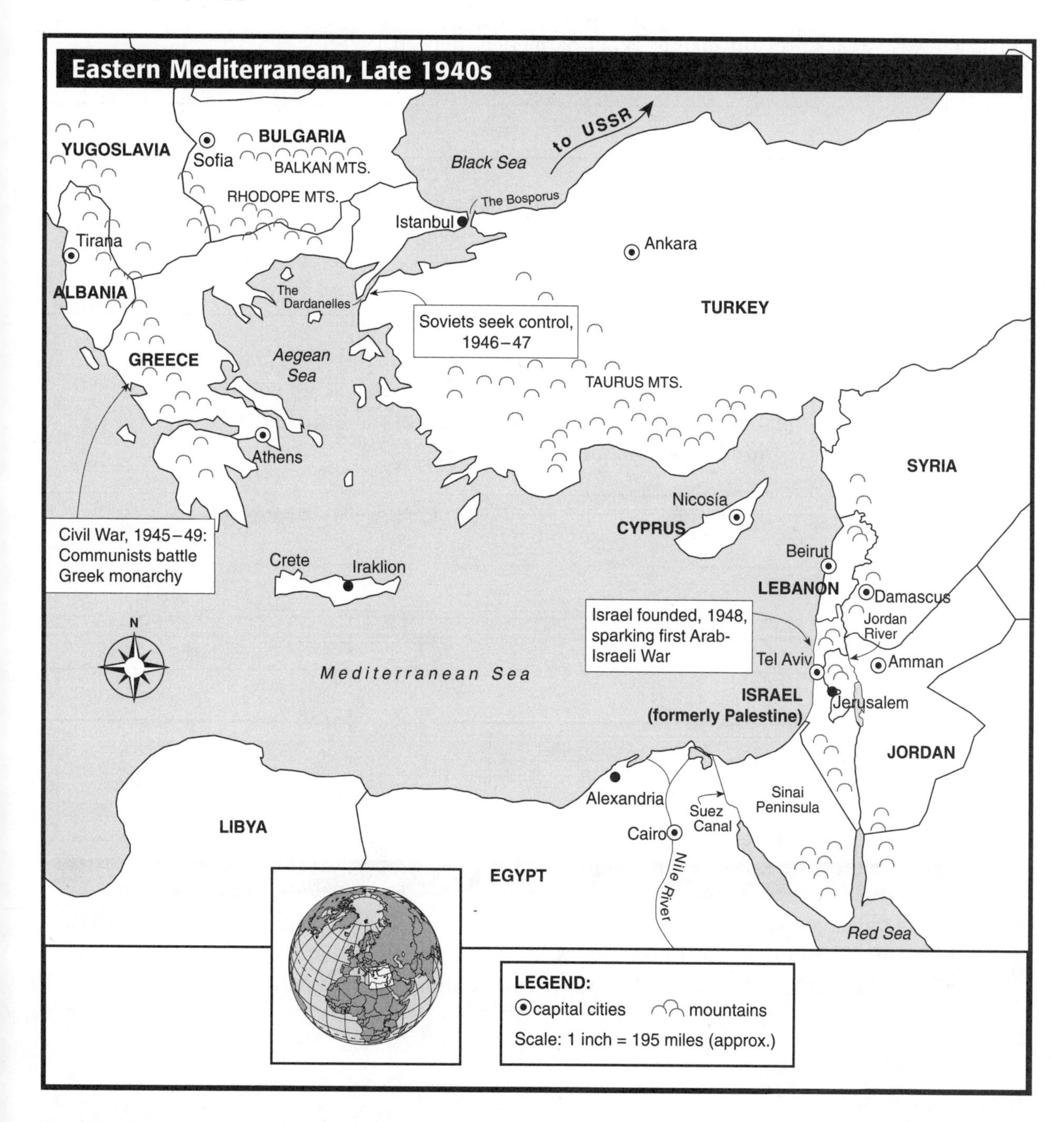

1. What mountains, rivers, and seas are named on this map? Where is the Nile River? Where is the Sinai Peninsula?

2. What countries and capital cities are shown on the map?

3. What was Israel's previous name? What happened there in 1948?

4. What two straits are located near Istanbul? In what country are they located?

5. **Critical Thinking: Human Systems** President Truman issued the Truman Doctrine partly in response to increasing Soviet pressure on Turkey to give up control of the Dardanelles. Why might the USSR have wanted to control the Dardanelles? Why might Truman have found this possibility threatening?

ACTIVITY

Draw a map of the same area of the world today, showing national boundaries. Use the color blue to show boundaries and country names that are the same today. Use red to show boundaries and country names that are different.

Name ____________ Class ________ Date ________

CHAPTER 20

Society After World War II

GEOGRAPHY ACTIVITY

Shifting Populations

As the two maps below show, between 1950 and 1960 the population of African Americans in the city of Chicago went through great changes. Mainly because of migration from the South, the population of African Americans in the city almost doubled, going from 492,265 to 812,637. Statistics also reveal another change: The percentage of African Americans increased in certain areas of the city. Several events caused this change. Many whites moved to suburbs, a shift that was taking place all over the United States. High-rise urban renewal projects also concentrated people in certain areas. In addition, prejudice was at work in Chicago, making it harder for African American families to either rent or buy housing in areas that were primarily white. Examine the map below, and answer the questions that follow.

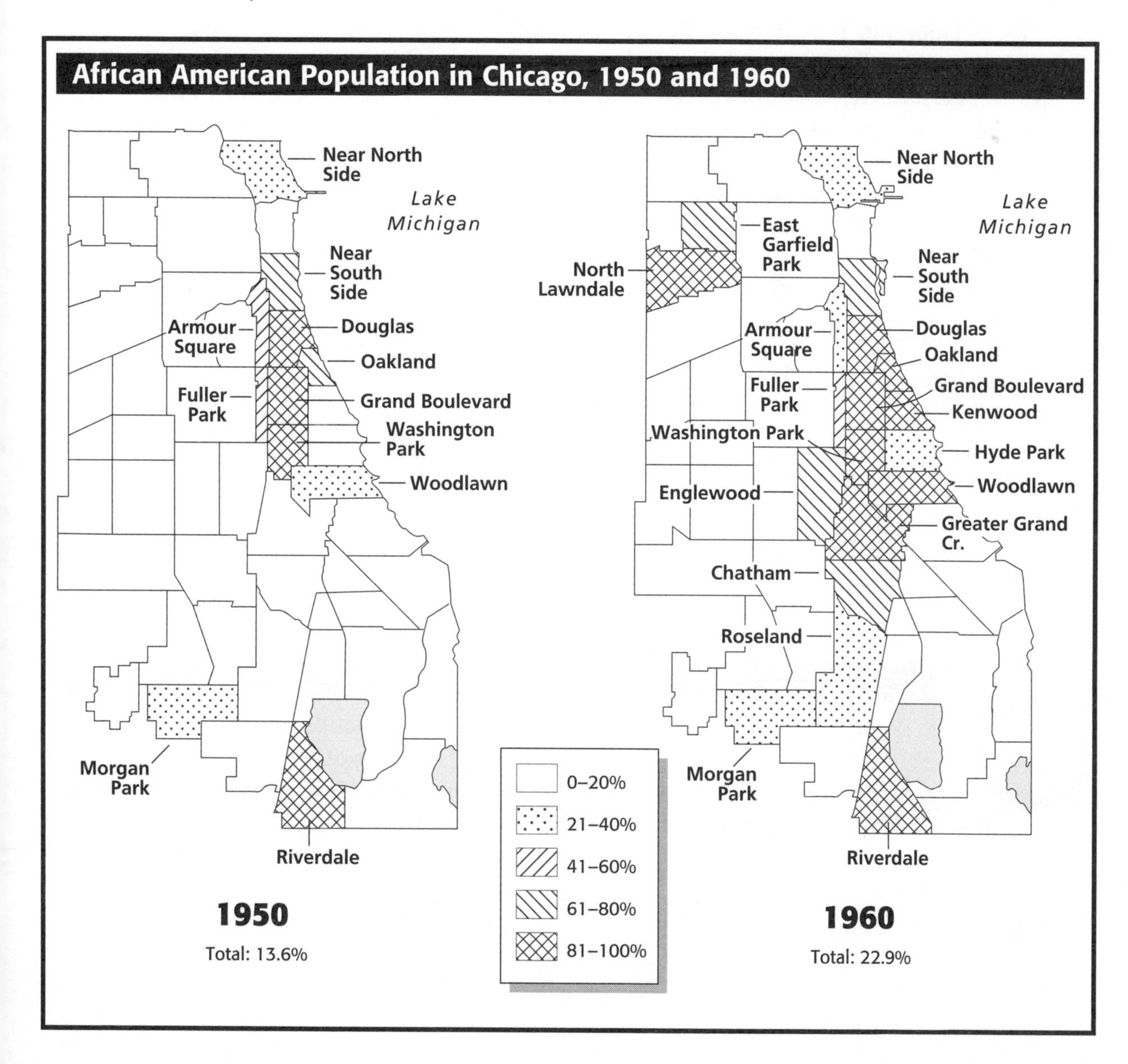

1. Which areas in 1950 had an African American population of 41–60 percent? In 1960?

____

2. Which areas in both 1950 and 1960 had an African American population of 81–100 percent?

____

3. Which area(s) underwent no change between 1950 and 1960?

____

4. Which area(s) went through the greatest change in the 10 years between 1950 and 1960? Explain your choice(s).

____

____

5. Critical Thinking: The World in Spatial Terms Analyzing a map can often tell you things about the lives of people living there. For instance, the area around Near North Side and Near South Side is the city's major downtown area, so many of the buildings there are devoted to businesses instead of living space. Many people who migrated to Chicago from the South in the 1950s were looking for employment in the factories and steel mills found in the Chicago area. Where do you think the major manufacturing areas were at that time? Explain your answer.

____

____

____

____

____

____

ACTIVITY

The population of the place where you live probably changed a great deal between 1950 and today. Research the population statistics of your town. Pick a ten-year period, and make two maps similar to the ones shown here. You may concentrate on various ethnic groups or on overall population.

Name ______________________ Class __________ Date __________

CHAPTER 21

The New Frontier and the Great Society

GEOGRAPHY ACTIVITY

The Cuban Missile Crisis

In October 1962, U.S. reconnaissance discovered a buildup of Soviet nuclear missiles in Cuba. President John F. Kennedy demanded that the Soviets remove the missiles and ordered a blockade of Cuba. A tense standoff between the United States and the Soviet Union followed, bringing the two superpowers to the brink of nuclear conflict. Shortly after Kennedy issued his ultimatum, Soviet leader Nikita Khrushchev backed down, removing the missiles and avoiding the confrontation. The map below shows the locations of the Soviet missile installations and the area of the Cuban blockade. Examine the map, and answer the questions about it that follow.

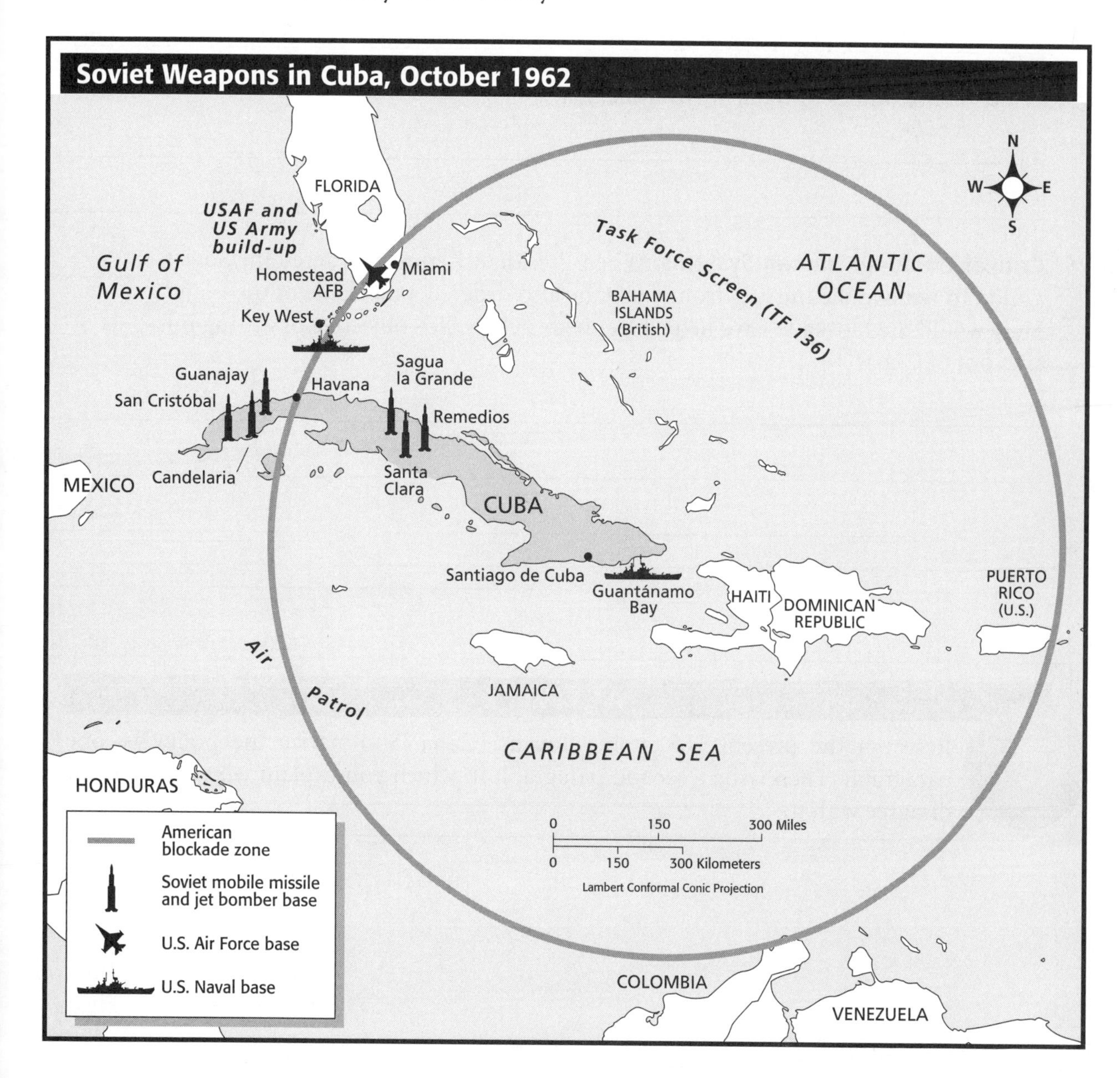

1. How many Soviet missile and jet bomber bases were in Cuba? On which part of the island were they located?

____

2. What type of U.S. military base was located in Cuba? On which part of the island was it located?

____

3. What countries other than Cuba were inside the U.S. blockade zone?

____

____

4. Which U.S. state is located closest to Cuba?

____

5. Which major bodies of water surround Cuba?

____

____

6. **Critical Thinking: Human Systems** When President Kennedy ordered the Soviet Union to remove the missiles from Cuba, he also ordered a blockade of the island. How would the blockade have helped Kennedy achieve his objective of getting missiles out of Cuba?

____

____

____

____

ACTIVITY

Research the present U.S. policy toward Cuba. Summarize the policy in one paragraph. Then write a second paragraph in which you explain why you agree or disagree with it.

Name ______ Class ______ Date ______

CHAPTER 22

The Civil Rights Movement

GEOGRAPHY ACTIVITY

The Civil Rights Movement

The civil rights movement was marked by many important events, ranging from peaceful demonstrations to violent race riots. Some of these events are noted on the map below. Examine the map, and answer the questions that follow.

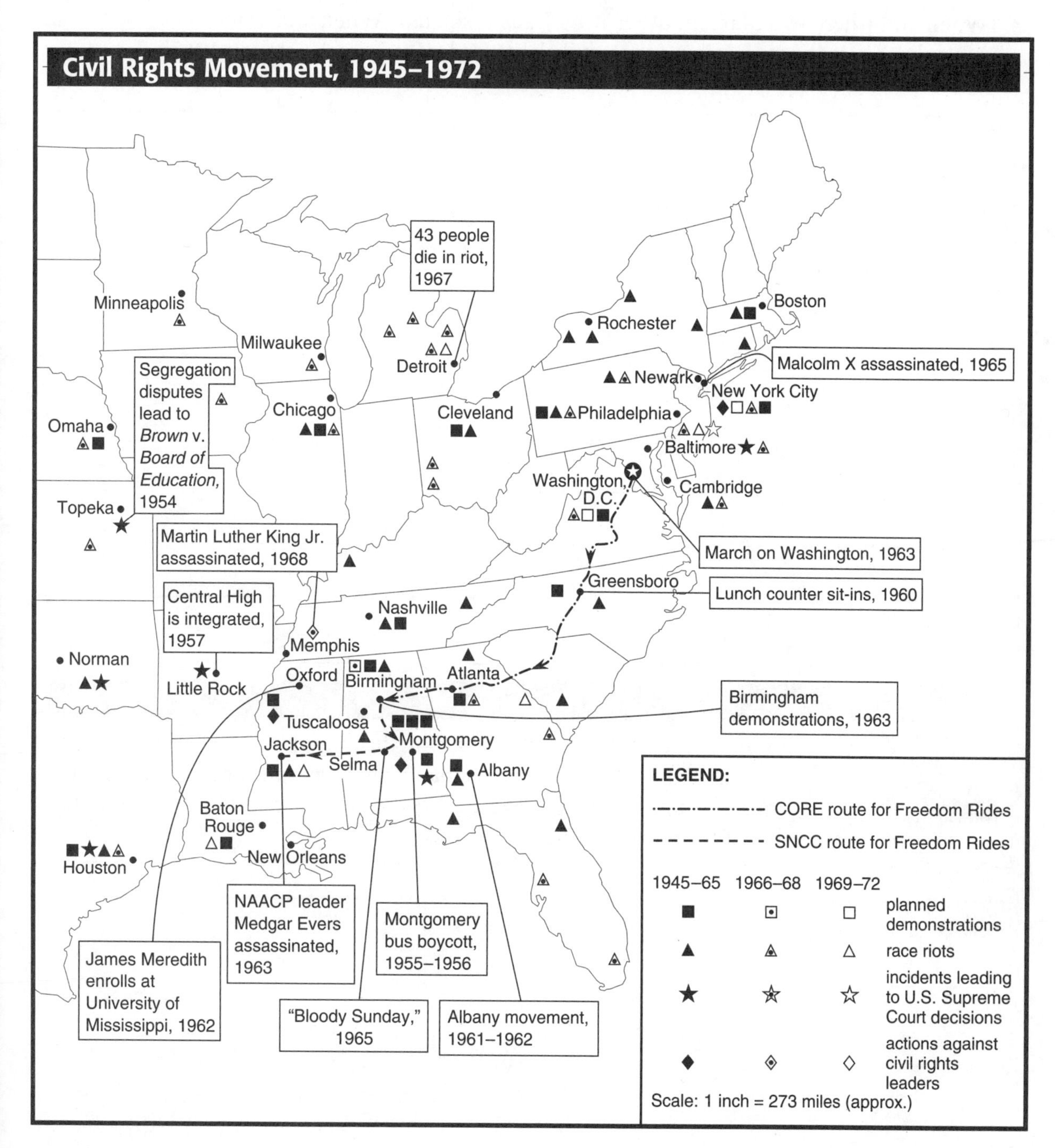

1. When did the Montgomery bus boycott take place?

2. What types of events occurred in Nashville, Tennessee?

3. What is the earliest event labeled on the map? What is the latest event?

4. When and where was Martin Luther King Jr. assassinated? When and where was Malcolm X assassinated? What other civil rights leader was assassinated in 1963?

5. **Critical Thinking: Places and Regions** According to the map, how did the type of events associated with the civil rights movement change from 1945 to 1972? Why might this change have occurred?

ACTIVITY

Imagine you are a reporter witnessing one of the important civil rights events shown on the map. Research to find out as many details as you can about the event; then, using an audiotape recorder, make an "on-the-scene" report of the event. Play your report (no more than 5 minutes) in class.

Name ______ Class ______ Date ______

CHAPTER 23

Struggles for Change

GEOGRAPHY ACTIVITY

The Environment Under Assault

When people hear that an animal is in danger of extinction, they often blame something such as overhunting or pollution, and sometimes they are right. However, biologists say that often the greatest danger is loss of habitat, or living space. In a developed nation like the United States, habitat is usually lost when cities expand, or sprawl, over land that once was farmland or forests. In developing countries such as Brazil, habitat is lost when forests are cut down to make room for farms. In any environment, once animals lose places to live or acquire food, their populations become smaller and smaller. Once a population becomes too small, extinction is almost unavoidable, and once any biological resource is lost, it cannot be replaced. The map below shows areas in the Americas where certain species are endangered. Study the map; then answer the questions that follow.

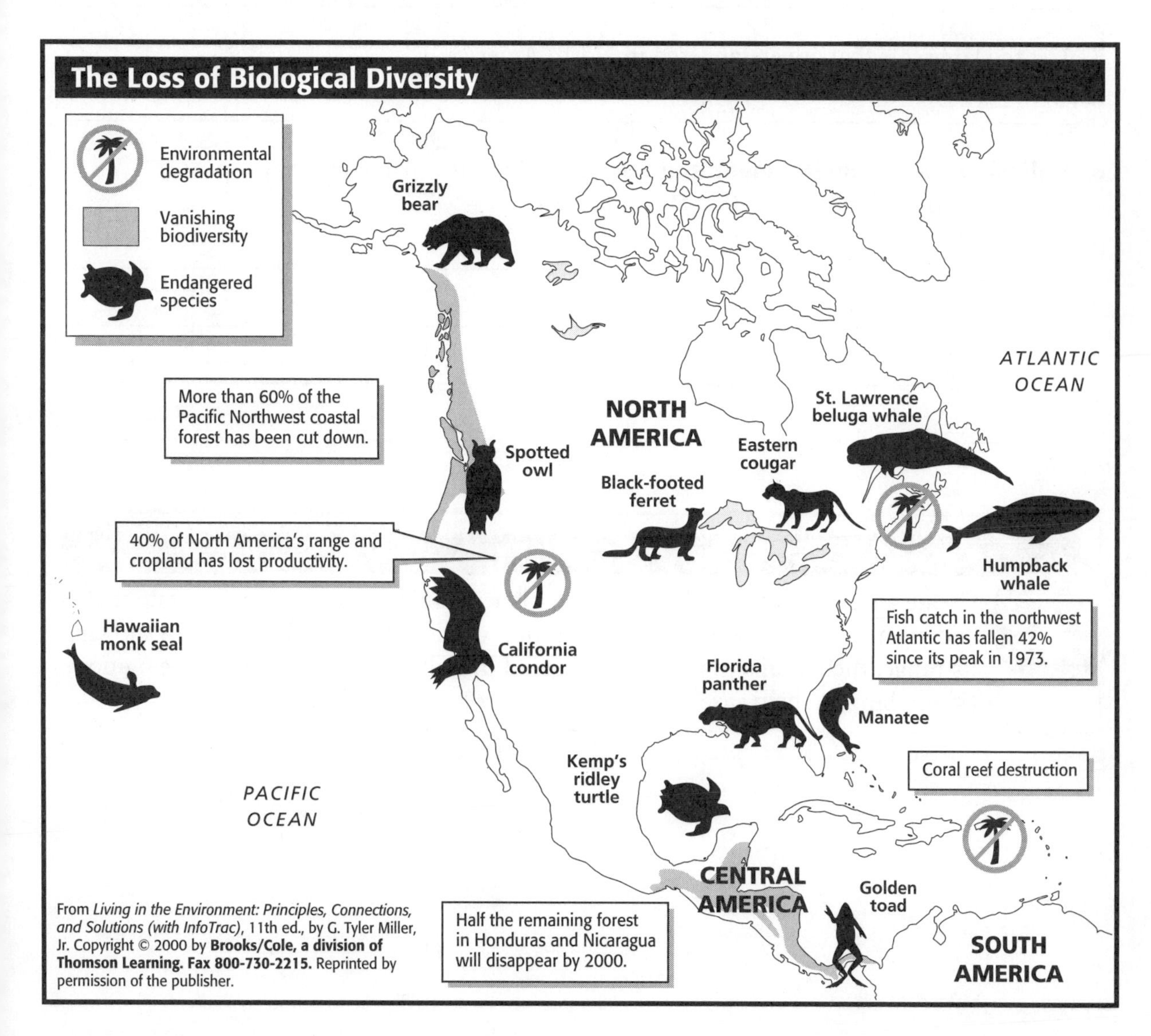

From *Living in the Environment: Principles, Connections, and Solutions (with InfoTrac)*, 11th ed., by G. Tyler Miller, Jr. Copyright © 2000 by **Brooks/Cole, a division of Thomson Learning. Fax 800-730-2215.** Reprinted by permission of the publisher.

1. What is the main type of habitat loss in Central America?

____

2. Which species is endangered in the northwestern part of North America?

____

3. What is the main environmental problem in the northwest Atlantic Ocean? What might cause such a problem?

____

____

____

4. Where is the major area of vanishing biodiversity in North America?

____

5. List the large cats that are endangered in North America.

____

6. Critical Thinking: Environment and Society Why is it worthwhile for people to save plant and animal species that are endangered?

____

____

____

____

ACTIVITY

Create a poster that tells the story of a plant or animal species in your state that is endangered. Include a photo or illustration of the plant or animal, a map showing its range, the reasons that it is endangered in bullet form, and what is being done (if anything) to help save it.

Name ______________________ Class __________ Date __________

War in Vietnam

GEOGRAPHY ACTIVITY

Geography and the Vietnam War

Geographic factors played an important part in the Vietnam War. The map below shows the main physical features of Vietnam. Examine the map, and answer the questions that follow.

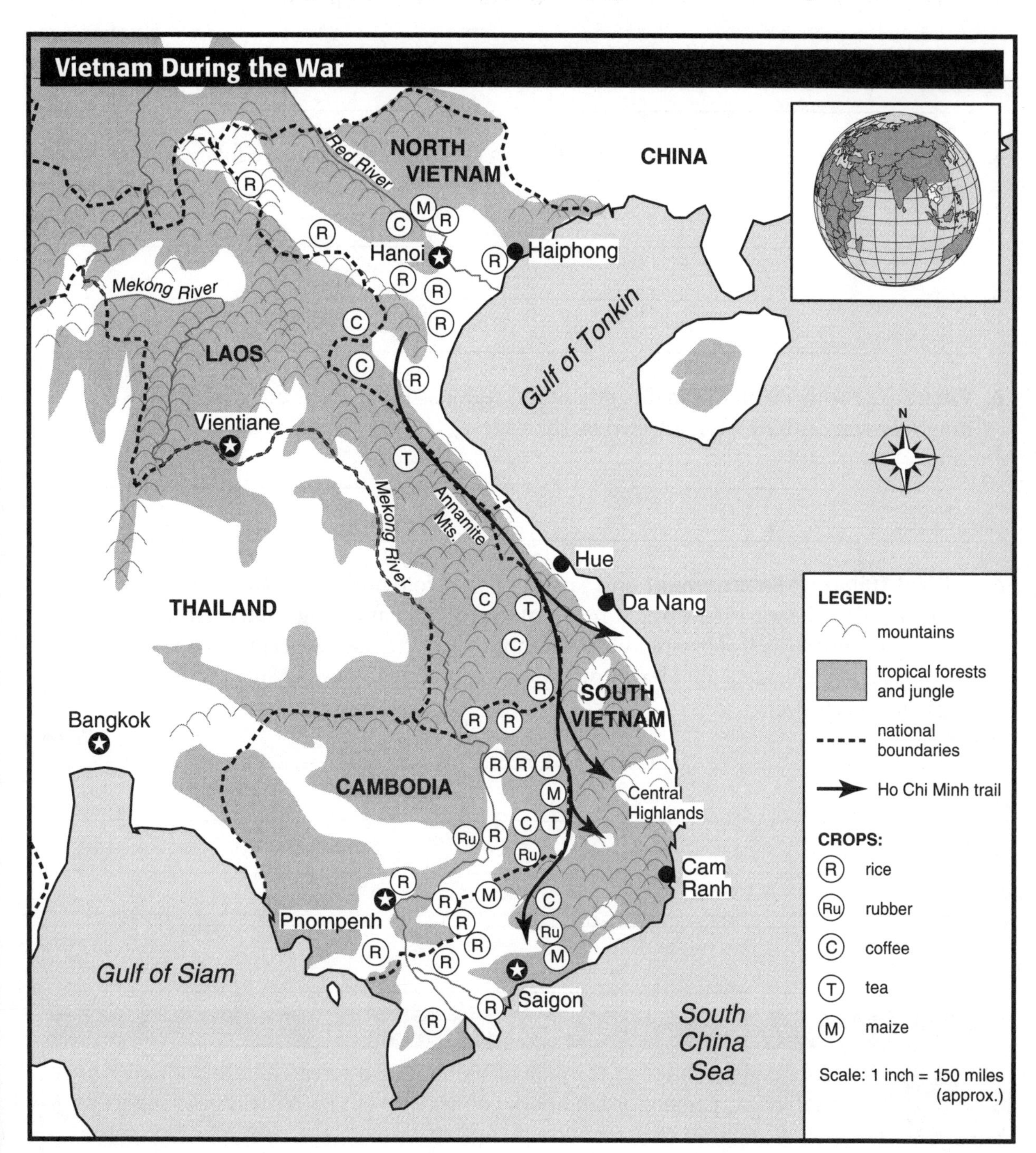

1. What rivers, mountainous regions, and cities are listed on the map?

____

____

2. In addition to mountains, what physical feature is common to much of Vietnam?

____

3. What countries border Vietnam? What bodies of water lie around it?

____

____

4. Describe the route of the Ho Chi Minh Trail. Why might the trail have followed that route?

____

____

____

5. Where are South Vietnam's main agricultural regions? What crops are grown? How might these areas have been affected by the war?

____

____

6. **Critical Thinking: Environment and Society** What role might Vietnam's geography have played in the war? How might mountainous terrain and jungle have affected military tactics? Which side would have been most able to use geography as an advantage? Which side would have considered geography to have been an obstacle? Explain your answer.

____

____

____

____

ACTIVITY

Choose one of the cities on the map of Vietnam. Do research to find a well-known historical event, person, or landmark connected with it. Write a brief report on it and include a photo or illustration if you can.

Name ______________________ Class __________ Date __________

CHAPTER 25

From Nixon to Carter

GEOGRAPHY ACTIVITY

Southern Africa in the 1970s

During the 1970s the Carter administration tried to reach out to newly independent states in Africa, hoping to win allies and limit the potential for Cold War conflict on the continent. Southern Africa—a region marked by civil war and the South African policy of apartheid, or racial segregation—was of special concern. The map below shows key developments in this region from 1970 to 1980. Examine the map, and answer the questions that follow.

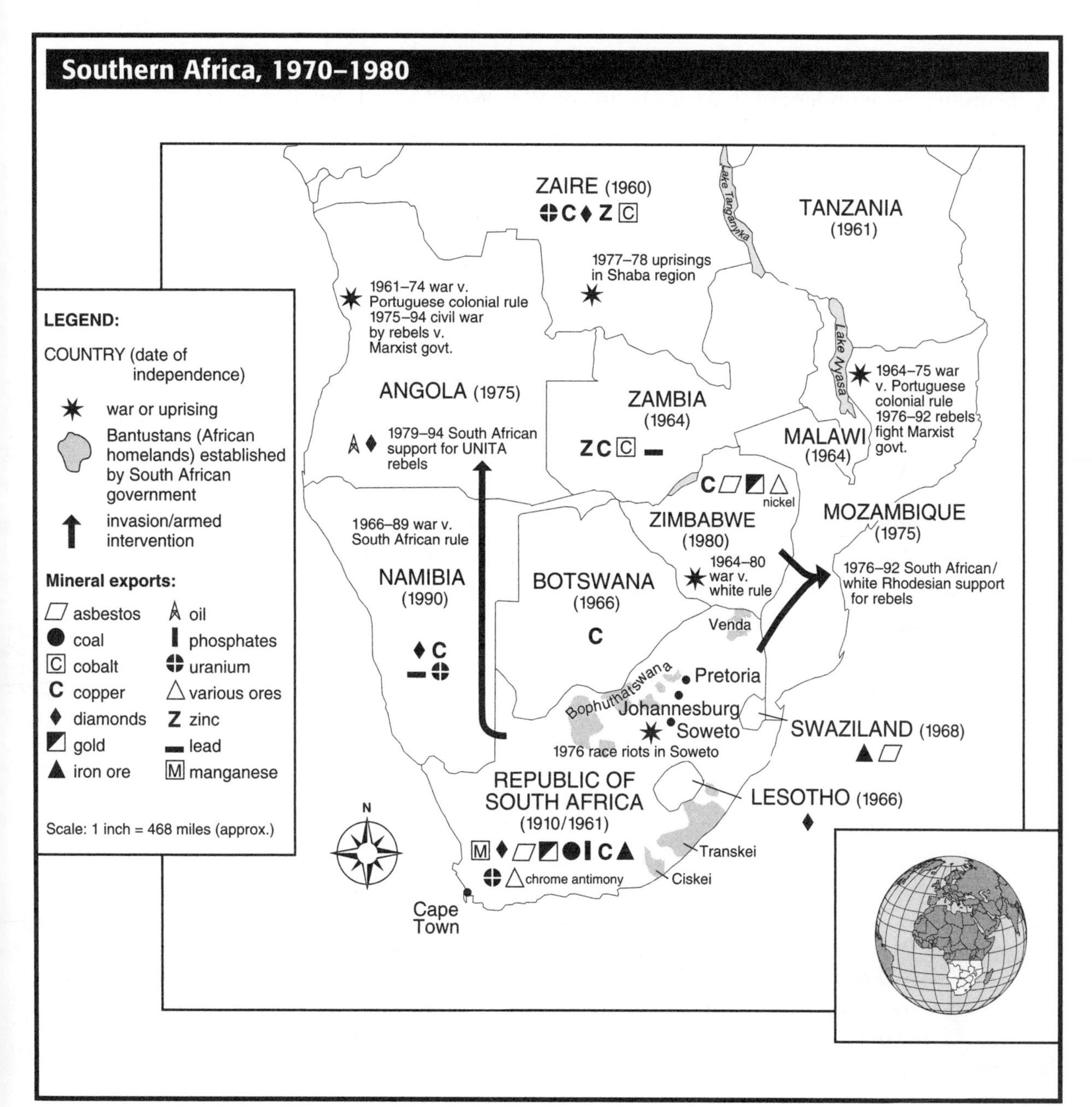

1. What countries are shown on this map? Which one is completely surrounded by the Republic of South Africa?

____

____

2. What two countries won their independence in 1975? What role has South Africa played in events in these countries?

____

____

3. Where is Zimbabwe located? When did it win independence?

____

4. Namibia came under South African control after World War I. What mineral resources did South Africa get from this colony? How and when did Namibia become independent?

____

____

5. What South African race riots are noted on the map? Where were they in relation to Johannesburg and to the Bantustan of Bophuthatswana?

____

____

6. Critical Thinking: Places and Regions South Africa's policy of apartheid was instituted in 1948. How might the variety of mineral resources and the political instability of southern Africa have encouraged U.S. policy makers to support South Africa in spite of the continuation of apartheid? What factors might account for new pressures on South Africa to end apartheid during Jimmy Carter's administration?

____

____

____

____

ACTIVITY

Draw a map of this area of southern Africa today. Pick one of the following themes for the map: physical features, transportation, ethnic or racial groups, major cities, population density, wildlife.

Name ________________ Class ________ Date ________

CHAPTER 26

The Republican Revolution

GEOGRAPHY ACTIVITY

The Arms Race

By the mid-1980s the United States and the Soviet Union had taken cautious steps to limit their nuclear arms race. Nevertheless, both sides still possessed enough nuclear weapons to destroy the world several times over, and other countries were developing nuclear arsenals of their own. The map below shows the extent of nuclear weapons stockpiles and capabilities in 1985. Examine the map, and answer the questions below.

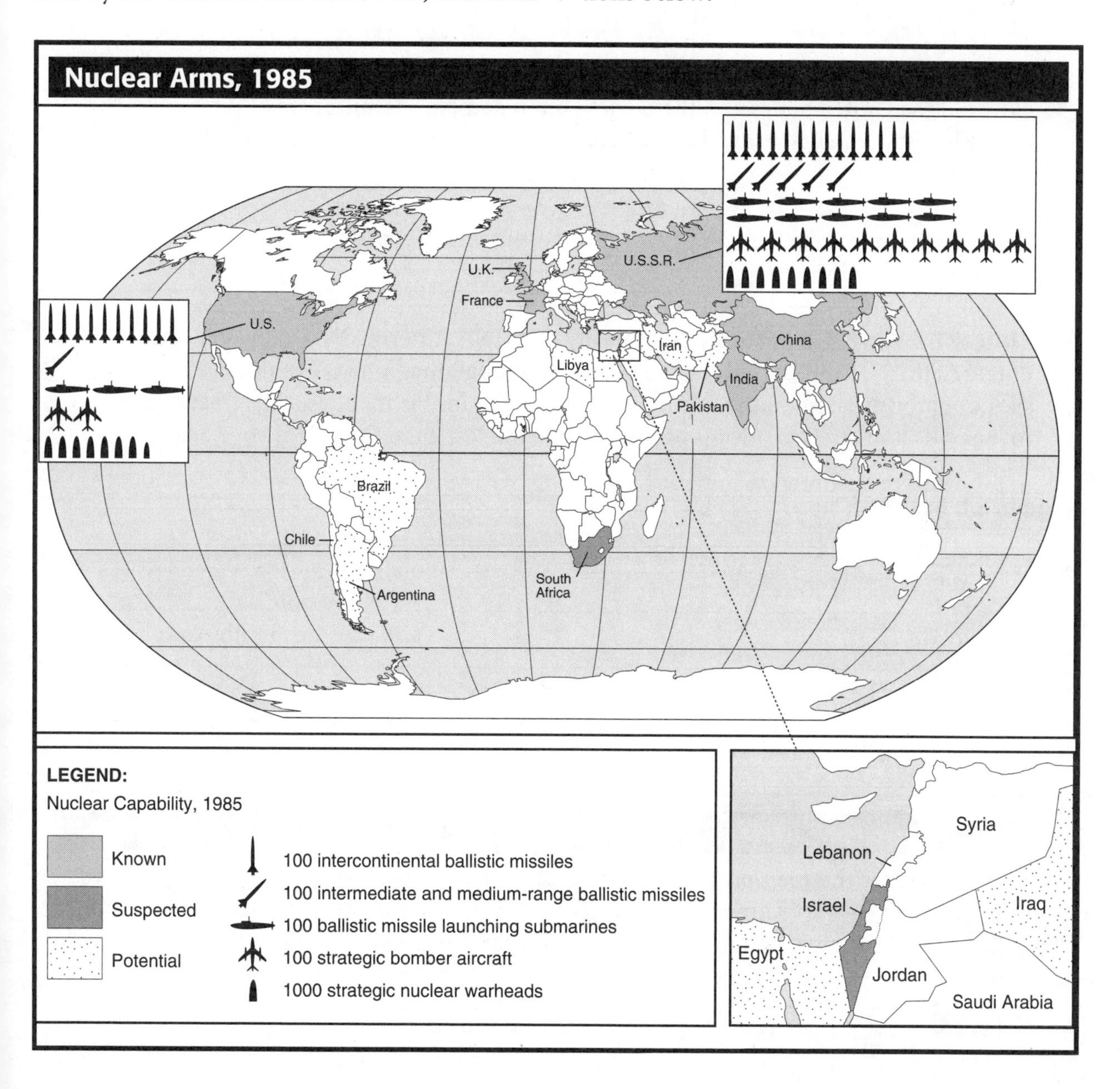

1. Which countries were known to have nuclear weapons capability in 1985?

___

2. Which countries were suspected of having nuclear weapons?

___

3. Which countries were thought to have the potential to make nuclear weapons?

___

4. Which region of the world contains the greatest number of nations that were known, suspected, or potential nuclear powers?

___

5. How did the United States and the Soviet Union compare in numbers of intercontinental ballistic missiles? How did they compare in numbers of strategic bomber aircraft?

___

___

6. **Critical Thinking: The Uses of Geography** The INF (Intermediate-range Nuclear Forces) Treaty of 1987 called for the elimination of all medium-range nuclear missiles in Europe. Based on the information presented in this map, was this treaty likely to have been an effective means of limiting the nuclear threat? Explain your answer.

___

___

___

___

___

ACTIVITY

Redraw the map on the worksheet so that it shows "Nuclear Arms" for this year. Color in the "Known," "Suspected," and "Potential" nuclear powers. Note countries that have joined the nuclear club since this map was drawn for 1985.

CHAPTER 27

Launching the New Millennium

GEOGRAPHY ACTIVITY

The Republicans Take the House

The midterm election of 1994 marked a new era in congressional politics. The Republicans won control of the Senate for the first time since 1986. They won control of the House for the first time in more than 40 years. Disenchantment with the status quo allowed Republicans to pick up seats all over the nation, especially in the South, which once had been solidly Democratic. The map below shows the breakdown by political party of all people elected to the House of Representatives in 1994. Examine the map, and answer the questions that follow.

The 1994 Election for U.S. House of Representatives

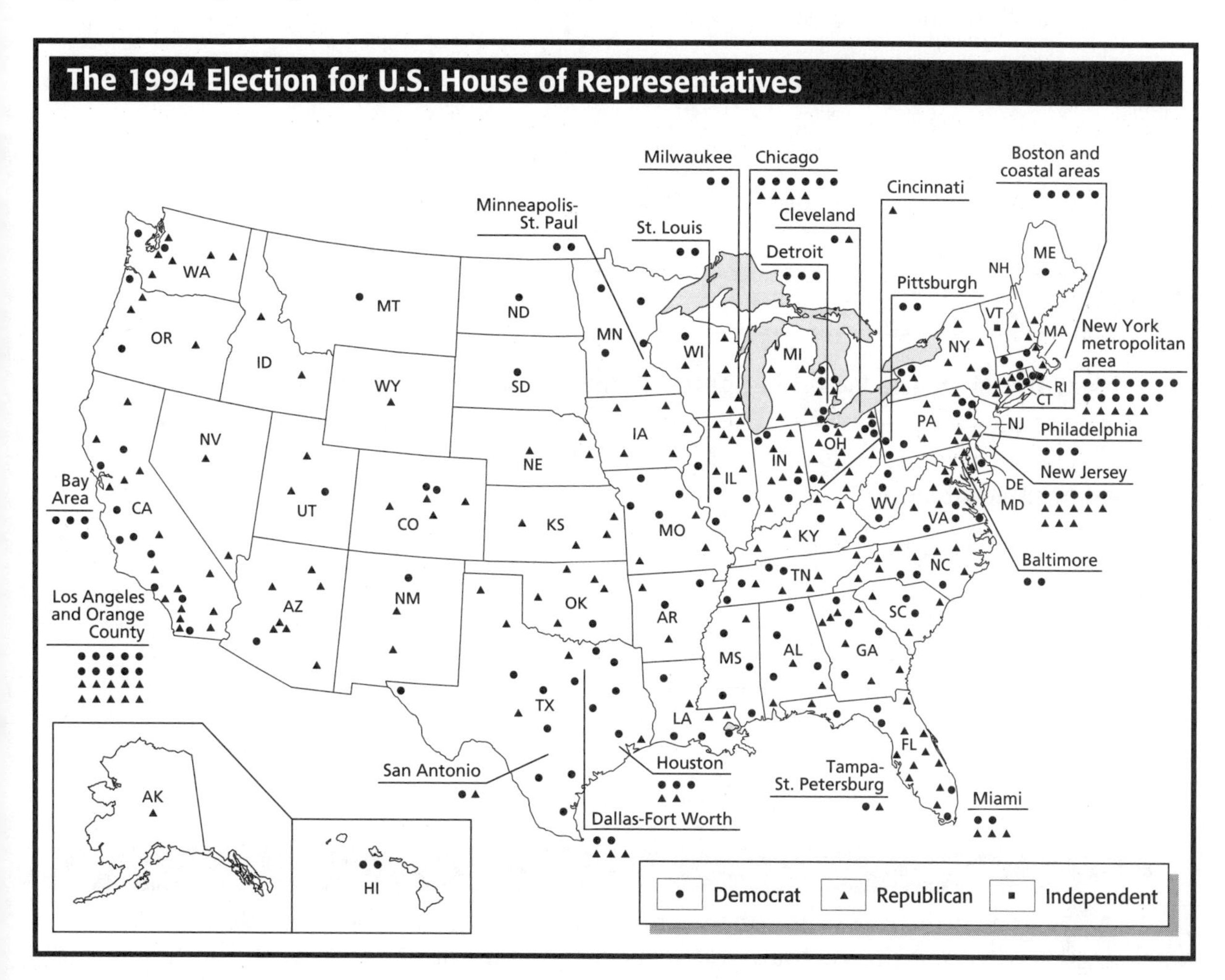

1. List the states that bucked the trend and elected only Democrats to the House.

____

2. Name the one state that elected an independent to the House.

____

3. In general, which area of the country has the fewest members of the House of Representatives? Why is this the case?

____

____

4. How many Republican congresspersons does your state have? How many Democratic ones does your state have?

____

____

5. Describe the representation of Maine after the 1994 election.

____

____

6. **Critical Thinking: The World in Spatial Terms** Only one representative out of 435 elected to the House in 1994 was an independent. What does that tell you about the political system in the United States? Express your opinion about whether this is a good or a bad situation.

____

____

____

____

ACTIVITY

Draw a map of your congressional district. Place your town within the district. Write the name of your congressperson and his or her party at the bottom of the map. Then contact your congressperson's office for literature that will tell you his or her stands on various issues. Based on what you learn, write a short essay explaining whether you would support this person with your vote and why.